RETHINKING FREIRE
Globalization and the Environmental Crisis

Sociocultural, Political, and Historical Studies in Education
Joel Spring, Editor

RETHINKING FREIRE

Globalization and the Environmental Crisis

Edited by

C. A. Bowers
University of Oregon

Frédérique Apffel-Marglin
Smith College

LEA
LAWRENCE ERLBAUM ASSOCIATES, PUBLISHERS
2005   Mahwah, New Jersey   London

Lawrence Erlbaum Associates, Inc., Publishers
10 Industrial Avenue
Mahwah, New Jersey 07430

Cover photos by Naomi Silverman.
Cover design by Kathryn Houghtaling Lacey.

Library of Congress Cataloging-in-Publication Data

Re-thinking Freire : globalization and the environmental crisis /
edited by C. A. Bowers, Frédérique Apffel-Marglin
   p.   cm.
Includes bibliographical references and index.
ISBN 0–8058–5114–3 (cloth : alk. paper)
ISBN 13: 978-0-8058-5114-4
   1. Developing countries—Economic conditions. 2. Globalization
—Economic aspects—Developing countries. 3. Environmental
degradation—Developing countries. 4. Globalization—Social aspects—
Developing countries. 5. Human ecology—Social aspects—Developing
countries. 6. Environmental education—Developing countries. 7. Freire,
Paulo, 1921– I. Bowers, C. A. II. Apffel-Marglin, Frédérique.
HC59.72.E5418 2004
337'.09172'4—dc22   2004040936

Printed in the United States of America
10 9 8 7 6 5 4 3 2 1

Contents

Preface

The title of this collection of essays by Third World activists, *Rethinking Freire: Globalization and the Environmental Crisis*, highlights two major world changes overlooked by Freire and his many followers: the Third World grassroots cultural resistance to economic globalization and the ecological crisis. The essays by Third World activists are important for a number of reasons. First, their criticisms of Freire's pedagogy are based on their attempts to combine consciousness raising with literacy programs in such diverse cultural settings as Bolivia, Peru, India, southern Mexico, and Cambodia. They discovered that Freire's pedagogy is based on Western assumptions that undermine indigenous knowledge systems. The field testing of Freire's pedagogy, which was carried out by local activists who were both personal friends of Freire and spoke the local languages, stands in sharp contrast to how Freire's ideas are presented in English-speaking universities and by professors in Third World universities who have received advanced degrees in Western universities. That is, the Third World activists recognized the colonizing nature of the cultural assumptions underlying his pedagogy, whereas the Western professors with only a reading knowledge of his writings continue to think of them as universally valid.

A second major limitation with Freire's ideas, reproduced in the writings of his followers, is that he ignored until just before his death the cultural implications of the ecological crisis. Recently, Moacir

Gadotti, the Director of the Instituo Paulo Freire in Brazil, urged educational reformers to understand that the chapter Freire wrote on the educational implications of the environmental crisis (for a book he was unable to finish because of his untimely death) establishes him as a leading theorist of an ecopedagogy. This pedagogy of the Earth, according to Gadotti (2000), must work for the creation of a new planetary citizenship—one that is based on a "unifying vision of the planet and a world society" (p. 8). Achieving this new planetary consciousness will require, as Gadotti extrapolates from previous Freire writings, eliminating "the transmission of culture from one generation to the next." That is, each generation is to create its own history by being critical of every aspect of daily life. Thus, the development of planetary citizenship will instead require educators to promote "the grand journey of each individual into the interior of his universe and in the universe that surrounds him." Although Freire's late acknowledgment of the ecological crisis is significant, it is even more important to understand that he did not recognize that the Western cultural assumptions that are the basis of his classic, *Pedagogy of the Oppressed*, cannot be reconciled with addressing the cultural roots of the ecological crisis. Unfortunately, Gadotti fails to recognize the imperialistic nature of the Freirean canon in his elaboration of a Freirean-based ecopedagogy. Thus, Freire's influence continues, with an educational reform agenda that is dedicated to the elimination of the cultural/linguistic diversity that is the basis of the world's biodiversity and that undermines the forms of intergenerational knowledge that are the basis of the diverse approaches to sustaining the local commons as sites of resistance to economic and technological globalization. The essays by the Third World activists represented in this book highlight Freire's failure to understand that his emancipatory vision is based on the same assumptions that underlie the planetary citizenship envisioned by the neoliberals promoting the Western model of global development. More importantly, the essays provide a glimpse into the diversity of cultural ways of knowing and their approaches to nurturing the commons that have been systematically excluded from the writings of Freire and his followers. And it is their descriptions that need to be considered in determining whether the efforts of Western educational reformers

are contributing to the revitalization of the commons or to undermining them in ways that further limit the prospects of current and
future generations.

OVERVIEW

Introduction
C. A. Bowers

This provides the background for bringing together the Third World
activists to share their experiences in using Freirean ideas in their
respective literacy programs, and to present papers that were later
expanded for the purposes of publishing a book that situates his ideas
within the larger context of global warming and Third World resistance to the Western model of development.

From a Pedagogy for Liberation to Liberation From Pedagogy
Gustavo Esteva, Dana L. Stuchul, Madhu Suri Prakash

This essay examines Freire's approach to liberating people from
oppression that represented an alternative to the armed struggle
advocated by Marxist theorists. Drawing on Esteva's long years of
working with indigenous cultures in southern Mexico, the authors
point out that Freire failed to understand the connections between
critical reflection as the only approach to knowledge and the promotion of a modern Western form of consciousness. Their essay
also questions the role Freire assigns to educators as intervention-
ists—particularly when they lack a deep knowledge of the culture
where they are intervening. The authors contrast Freire's approach
to empowerment with the more community-centered and intergenerational approaches found in indigenous cultures. Another strength
of the chapter is the ability of the authors to place Freire's ideas in
the context of the revolutionary thinking that was sweeping through
Third World countries.

Nurturance in the Andes
Grimaldo Rengifo Vasquez

Rengifo, founder of PRATEC (the Andean Project for Peasant Technologies), describes his early experiences in using Freire's literacy
program with the indigenous people of northern Peru. He provides
a detailed description of how the peasants responded to the different steps in clarifying the difference between culture and nature, as
well as the peasants' response to the introduction of abstract thinking—which is part of a literacy-based form of consciousness. Rengifo
then contrasts the form of individualism fostered by Freire's literacy
program, with its emphasis on an individualized perspective and its
separation of humans from nature, with the Quechua worldview.
Rengifo gives particular emphasis to how the Quechua understand
the connections between the deities, nature, and humans—and how
all relationships are nurturing relationships. This comparison brings
out the fundamental differences between the Western cultural assumptions of Freire's model of thinking and the Quechua worldview
that has produced one of the world's most diverse and productive
traditions of agriculture.

Who Are the Oppressed?
Barbara Loyda Sanchez Bejarano

Before and following her exile for her revolutionary activities, Loyda
Sanchez was involved in the Popular Education programs that were
based on Freire's pedagogical methods. In addition to describing
how foreign the process of dialectical thinking (which is the basis of
Freire's idea of critical reflection) was to the peasants' way of thinking, she explains how Freirean ideas continue the tradition of Marxist thinking that represents the peasants as unable to understand the
nature of their own oppressed condition. Her experience led to the
recognition that she was in fact engaged in a colonizing process, and
that she was the source of a new form of oppression. Her ability to
speak the local language led to the awareness that the peasant sense
of community did not involve the forms of hierarchy implicit in the
Freirean model of literacy, where the educator's role is to raise the

consciousness of the peasants. Rather, she found that their sense of community involved reciprocal responsibilities, and that they were not oppressed. Her chapter concludes with a discussion of the rural Bolivian peasant's approach to community, and the acknowledgment that her indoctrination into Western assumptions was the source of her own oppression.

Vernacular Education for Cultural Regeneration: An Alternative to Paulo Freire's Vision of Emancipation
Gustavo Terán

Terán describes how his early years as a Chicano activist were influenced by the ideas of Freire, and how his experience in working in the vernacular education programs in communities in the Oaxaca region of Mexico led him to recognize that community renewal and the basis of self-sufficiency could not be achieved through the strategy of teaching each generation to rename the world—as Freire advocated. Terán argues that the intergenerational renewal and sharing of knowledge, rather than the emancipation of the individual through critical reflection, is now more representative of social reform movements in southern Mexico. And unlike Freire's vision of uplifting all cultures through the adoption of critical reflection as the primary approach to knowledge, Terán argues that the renewal of vernacular knowledge as narrative traditions is essential to maintaining cultural diversity.

From Conscientization to Interbeing
Siddhartha

Siddhartha gives an account of the influence that Freire's ideas had on his thinking over a period of 25 years, and how his attempts to use them as the basis for emancipating tribal groups in southern India led him to the recognition that even though Freire was still a source of inspiration, his ideas were based on faulty assumptions. Siddhartha's chief criticism of Freirean thinking is that it is ethnocentric in that it does not recognize the practical and spiritual wisdom of cultural groups—even those at the bottom of India's class system. Siddhartha gives a poignant account of how the thinking of social activists in India has changed in recent years, as exemplified by the fact that he could no longer locate a copy of Freire's *Pedagogy of the Oppressed* among his colleagues or find it among his own books. The Western model of emancipation from oppressed conditions, he claims, has now been replaced by a renewed interest in Gandhi's approach to local traditions of community renewal. He concludes by noting the irony of the special status still accorded to Freire's ideas in colleges of education in English-speaking countries.

Whose Oppression is This? The Cultivation of Compassionate Action
Phyllis Robinson

Robinson's study of Buddhism, as well as her years of working with Buddhist nuns and other women in Cambodia, are the basis of her reflections on the contradictions in Freire's pedagogy. She describes how her own graduate studies were based on an uncritical and sustained encounter with Freire's ideas, which is followed by her discussion of how the application of these ideas in the Buddhist context of Cambodia led to her realization that Freire was a deeply Western thinker. The main contribution of her chapter is the account she gives of how her role in carrying out Freire's pedagogical model put her in conflict with the basic beliefs of the Buddhist women she was attempting to liberate—who understood liberation in an entirely different way. She concludes, like the other contributors who attempted to utilize Freirean ideas in non-Western settings, that she was the oppressor—and that an outsider cannot be the source of liberation.

Cease to Do Evil, Then Learn to Do Good (A Pedagogy for the Oppressor)
Derek Rasmussen

Rasmussen contrasts Freire's argument that indigenous cultures are incapable by themselves of recognizing their oppressed condition

(Freire identifies them as in a state of "intransitive consciousness") with the depth of knowledge of the Inuit people he has lived with for the last 12 years. In addition to providing a description of Inuit wisdom and practical knowledge, he discusses the differences between oral and literacy-based cultures. He points out that Freire's ideas need to be understood as an expression of a literacy-based form of consciousness, and that Freire and his followers ignore the fundamental differences. Freire's failure to understand these differences, as well as his narrow view of how knowledge is attained and renewed, led him (according to Rasmussen) to adopt a "rescuer" mentality. Rasmussen makes a strong case that the "rescuers" are the problem in terms of undermining the self-sustaining capabilities of the Inuit.

How the Ideas of Paulo Freire Contribute to the Cultural Roots of the Ecological Crisis
C. A. Bowers

Bowers argues that Freire and his followers share a number of the same deep cultural assumptions that gave conceptual and moral legitimacy to the Industrial Revolution and, now, to globalizing its digital phase. These assumptions include the idea that change is inherently progressive and linear in nature, that the individual is the basic social unit and source of critical judgment, that this is an anthropocentric world, and that all cultures should adopt a literacy-based form of critical intelligence. The chapter points out that although Freire was critical of capitalism as a source of exploitation, his emphasis on critical reflection as the only source of knowledge and on the need to overturn all traditions not only undermines the possibility of cultural diversity, which is necessary to sustaining biodiversity, it also leads to undermining the intergenerational knowledge that represents, in many cases, alternatives to a consumer-dependent society. Freire, in effect, argues for the emancipated individual without realizing that the emancipated individual (that is, one free of the network of mutual aid and moral reciprocity, as well as the knowledge and skills learned in mentoring relationships) is exactly the kind of individual that will be more dependent on consumerism to meet daily needs.

Afterword
C. A. Bowers

The "Afterword" presents a more balanced and culturally informed understanding of the education reforms that must be undertaken if we are to live within the sustaining capacity of natural systems. In addition to presenting a critique of economic globalization and the dangers of a world monoculture based on Western assumptions, the point is made that valuing critical reflection goes back to the time of Socrates and thus should not be associated with Freire as though he came up with the idea. The Afterword is also used to explain how intelligence is cultural rather than individualistic in nature, and how language carries forward deep cultural assumptions—causing people to think in many of the same patterns of earlier generations. Thinking of change as inherently progressive is one of these patterns that now needs to be challenged if we are to address one of the root causes of the ecological crisis. The argument is made that we must now ask what needs to be conserved that strengthens community and reduces our dependence on consumerism to meet daily needs—a process that is accelerating the decline in the viability of natural systems. It also points out that understanding that not all traditions are oppressive provides the basis for beginning the process of democratizing technology, as this process requires an understanding of what traditions will be lost through the introduction of new technologies. The "Afterword" also explains the nature of ecojustice and why it should be the focus of educational reform.

REFERENCE

Gadotti, M. (2000). *Pedagogy of the earth and culture of sustainability.* São Paulo, Brazil: Instituo Paulo Freire.

About the Editors
and Contributors

Frédérique Apffel-Marglin is Professor of Anthropology and Smith College, where she also directs the Center for Mutual Learning. She has been collaborating with the Peruvian organization PRATEC and its satellite grassroots organizations for the past 8 years. Prior to that she did ethnographic fieldwork in eastern India, focusing on gender, religion, and critiques of development. She has published seven books. The most recent are: *Dominating Knowledge: Development, Culture, and Resistance*, edited with S. A. Marglin (1990), and *Colonizing Knowledge: From Development to Dialogue*, with S. A. Marglin (1996). With PRATEC, she published *The Spirit of Regeneration: Andean Culture Confronting Western Notions of Development* (1998).

C. A. Bowers has been on the faculty of Portland State University and the University of Oregon, and is now Adjunct Professor of Environmental Studies at the University of Oregon. In addition to lecturing widely in the United States and foreign countries, he has published 15 books that address the cultural roots of the ecological crisis, with particular emphasis on how public schools and universities reproduce the mind-set that is now being globalized. His most recent books include *Educating for an Ecologically Sustainable Culture* (1995), *The Culture of Denial* (1997), *Let Them Eat Data* (2000), *Educating* *for Eco-Justice and Community* (2001), *Detras de la Apariencia* (2002), and *Mindful Conservatism* (2003).

Gustavo Esteva has served as a public servant, university professor, and, for the past 20 years, grassroots activist working with Indian groups, peasants, and the urban marginalized. The many posts he has held include President of the Fifth World Congress on Rural Sociology, Interim Chairman of the United National Research Institute for Social Development Board, and President of the Mexican Society for Planning. In addition to authoring over 200 articles and a dozen books, he has coauthored (with Madhu Suri Prakash) *Grassroots Modernism: Remaking the Soil of Culture* (1998), and *Escaping Education: Living and Learning Among Grassroots Cultures* (1998).

Madhu Suri Prakash is Professor of Education at Pennsylvania State University and the recipient of the Eisenhower Award for Distinguished Teaching. She received her PhD in Philosophy of Education from Syracuse University. In addition to publishing numerous articles, she has coauthored two books with Gustavo Esteva.

Grimaldo Rengifo Vasquez holds a Bachelor of Education degree from the Universidad Nacional del Centro, and went on to study anthropology at the Pontificia Universidad Catolica del Peru. He is currently codirector of PRATEC, which he founded in 1987. Prior to that he held various posts in government and international organizations. He also worked as a trainer at the Centro Nacional de Investigacion y Capacitacion para la Reforma Agraria at the Peruvian Ministry of Agriculture, and it was in this capacity that he attempted to use Freire's method of popular education. This was followed by serving as the Executive Director of an international rural development project funded by the Dutch government. He is the author of numerous books and essays in Spanish.

Derek Rasmussen is a Buddhist teacher and has lived in Iqaluit, Nunavut, since 1991. He recently served as a social and educational policy advisor to Nunavut Tunngavik, Inc. (NTI), the organization that represents the interests of the Inuit of Nunavut within the context of the Canadian political system. He has published a number of articles that address environmental and peace issues and differences in cultural ways of knowing. He also has lectured on these issues at several Canadian and American universities, and has been active in the peace movement in Canada.

Phyllis Robinson is the Director of Courageous Crossing, an organization based in Amherst, Massachusetts, that provides meditation retreats for international development workers. She spent 10 years working with women in Cambodia and, prior to that, in the refugee camps on the Thai–Cambodian border. Her training in Freirean approaches to education came from her doctoral work at the Center for International Education at the University of Massachusetts.

Loyda Sanchez studied economics at the Universidad Mayor de San Andres in La Paz, Bolivia, and later studied pedagogy in Cochabamba. In the early 1970s, she was a militant in the ELN, the army founded by Che Guevara. This resulted in incarceration and exile successively to Chile, Argentina, and Peru. On her return to Bolivia, she worked from 1980 until 1990 with indigenous peasant communities in the Cochabamba region using Freire's methodology of Popular Education. She is currently coordinator of CAIPACHA, an NGO (non-governmental organization) dedicated to Andean/Amazonian cultural affirmation and decolonization.

Siddartha studied law in India and anthropology at the Sorbonne in Paris. From 1978 to 1984, he was the Asian and then international coordinator of Freirean pedagogical methods in Third World countries. He founded several organizations in India and in Europe, including the South-North Network of Cultures and Development. He also founded, in India, the Institute for Cultural Research (a training institute for social activists using Freirean methods of consciousness raising), and Fedina (a field organization working in 15 tribal and peasant villages in South India). He is currently the Asia-Pacific coordinator of the Alliance for a Responsible and United World. His writings have appeared in the international press and in books.

Dana L. Stuchul is Assistant Professor in the Department of Educational Studies at Berea College, Berea, Kentucky. She received her PhD in Educational Theory and Policy from Pennsylvania State University in 1999. She is currently working on a book that examines the relevance of Ivan Illich's social critique. Her other research interests include the connections between modernity and technology.

Gustavo A. Terán recently earned his doctoral degree in Educational Leadership and Policy Studies from the University of Vermont and is now a Rockefeller Fellow at the University Center for International Studies at the University of North Carolina in Chapel Hill. While at the University of Vermont, he taught field-based courses on education, culture, and community development in Oaxaca, Mexico. His current research explores the relationship between the politics of cultural identity and the growing influence of the Western model of development.

Introduction

C. A. Bowers

The conference titled "Freire and Beyond" was held at Smith College and the University of Massachusetts (Amherst campus) in the fall of 2000, the same year the scientific community reached consensus that human behavior was a major contributor to global warming. Frédérique Apffel-Marglin, an anthropologist at Smith College, invited activists who had attempted to utilize Freire's pedagogy in Third World cultures, along with several others whose experience with non-Western cultures enabled them to recognize the Western assumptions that are the basis of Freire's ideas. The conference was organized partly in support of Third World efforts to resist further Western colonization in this era of ecological decline, and partly out of a concern with the way colleges of education in North America promote the different genres of liberal thinking that underlie current efforts to globalize a consumer-dependent lifestyle that is ecologically unsustainable. That Freire's followers represent him as a critic of these traditions of educational liberalism, whereas more thoughtful observers consider his ideas as supportive of core liberal assumptions, makes it especially important at this time to examine the assumptions that his followers have taken for granted.

The conference was remarkable for several reasons. First, it brought together a group of Third World activists who had spent many years working in popular literacy programs and in other consciousness-raising reform efforts. These activists initially were inspired social reformers with backgrounds very different from Western educational theorists who continue to promote Freire's ideas in colleges of education. They spoke the local languages and, in many cases, were members of the cultural group they initially set out to transform through Freire's literacy and consciousness-raising program. They were also careful observers of the local traditions of knowledge and patterns of mutual support. The papers presented at the conference, as well as several others that were subsequently invited, are thus based on years of experience in attempting to apply Freire's ideas in a diverse range of cultures, Because of the profound differences between how Third World social activists view Freire's ideas and how he is represented by educational theorists who promote his ideas based only on their personal relationship with him and on reading his books, it was decided that the conference papers should be presented to a larger audience in the form of a book.

Second, the conference papers document the transformation in the thinking of these Third World activists. They were at first deeply motivated by Freire's vision of empowerment, which they initially interpreted as a noncolonizing pedagogy. But as they learned from indigenous cultures, they became aware that Freire's ideas are based on Western assumptions and that the Freirean approach to empowerment was really a disguised form of colonization. The reflections on the strengths and weaknesses of Freire's pedagogy presented at the conference, and now available here, are thus the outgrowth of grounded experience profoundly different from the purely theoretically based interpretations that students encounter in colleges of education. The importance of this difference cannot be overemphasized. Reading *Pedagogy of the Oppressed*, as well as reading and listening to professors of education who have been personally close to Freire but have not tried to apply his ideas in different non-Western settings, can turn graduate students and other professors into what the late Eric Hoffer called the "true believer." Unfortunately, the messianic motivation to empower the oppressed and illiterate, as the chapters in this volume point out, is based on a lack of understanding and appreciation of the knowledge of the indigenous cultures.

Freire's emphasis on identifying the generative themes of a cultural group as the starting point in a literacy/consciousness-raising program appears, on the surface, to guarantee that his approach to empowerment avoids any form of outside cultural imposition. The problem is that Freire and his interpreters did not recognize the Western assumptions implicit in his understanding of what it means to be human, to be emancipated from the knowledge of previous generations, and to exist in ways that do not take account of the fate of the environment. Nor did Freire and his followers understand the complexity of orally based cultures and the differences in their way of knowing and encoding knowledge of community-supportive relationships. Indeed, Freire once referred to orality as "regressive illiteracy" and the oral cultures living in the interior of Brazil as the "backward regions of Brazil." Literacy for Freire and his followers was essential to becoming a critically reflective thinker and thus fully human. By ignoring a significant body of scholarly writings on the differences between orality and literacy, Freirean thinkers failed to understand that literacy itself is a colonizing process that reinforces a modern sense of individualism, privileges sight over the other senses, and fosters abstract thinking that is integral to critical reflection.

The timing of the conference was also important. Unlike previous scientific reports on changes in the chemistry of the oceans, the world-wide loss of topsoil, and the shortage of potable water, many segments of the public and even some politicians are now taking seriously the growing evidence of global warming. The changes in people's lives, as well as ecosystems that are being affected by global warming, have even led some heads of corporations to realize that the old paradigm that made profits the major concern must now change. As the contributors to this volume point out, although Freire shared many of Marx's criticisms of capitalism, he was unable to think in ways not dependent on the same assumptions that underlie the Western approach to economic development. Freire's assumptions about the linear and progressive nature of change, his understanding of critical reflection as the only valid approach to knowledge and as the basis of individual freedom, and his way of universalizing his revolutionary prescriptions in a way that ignores that there are over 5,000 languages still spoken in the world are echoed in current arguments for a global culture based on Western science, technology, and a consumer-dependent lifestyle. Freire's silence about the nature of the ecological crisis is also shared by the advocates of globalizing the Western mind-set and lifestyle. The American promoters of Freire's ideas—Henry Giroux, Peter McLaren, Donaldo Macedo, Ira Shor, and Svi Shapiro among others—reproduce in their writings the same silence. Although their writings are viewed as the radical canon within colleges of education, they now represent, in light of the ecological crisis, a reactionary way of thinking. Their criticisms of capitalism and the social roots of racism, class, and gender discrimination do not invalidate this criticism. Today, reactionary thinkers continue to embrace ideas and values that perpetuate the double bind implicit in an approach to progress that undermines the viability of the Earth's natural systems. To put this another way, the cultural assumptions that Freire and his followers continue to uphold as the basis of future change are the same core assumptions that undelie several hundred years of Western colonization and environmental devastation. They are, in effect, asking us to embrace the Western myths now being rejected in Third World cultures and by the more thoughtful environmentalists.

Our tradition of misusing our political categories makes it necessary to clarify further what now constitutes reactionary thinking. Academics and the general public often equate suggestions that indigenous cultures have developed sophisticated knowledge of local ecosystems and patterns of community interdependence with reactionary or romantic thinking. For them (and for Freire and John Dewey), cultures have evolved from a prerational state of existence (i.e., indigenous) to the higher state of complexity marked by literacy, critical reflection, and individualism. This evolutionary framework of thinking was a key part of the ideology that justified the last hundred-plus years of Western colonization. If we are to break with this tradition, it will be necessary to avoid judging the Third World activists represented in this book as either reactionary or romantic. Like many other Third World writers, they understand the importance of maintaining linguistic diversity as a basis for resisting globalization, which has not been part of an evolutionary interpretation of cultural development. They also understand the vital connections between linguistic diversity and biodiversity. The different indigenous ways of knowing, which are adapted in ways that take account of the characteristics of the local bioregions, are also the basis of mutual aid and intergenerational knowledge that contributes to self-sufficiency.

Modern thinkers in the Freire and Dewey tradition will claim that the efforts of these activists to revitalize local cultural traditions of self-sufficiency are the real expression of reactionary thinking. But this is not the case. They are not attempting to revive traditions that are environmentally disruptive. More importantly, they are not attempting to reestablish traditions that have disappeared. Rather, as Vandana Shiva points out, community and more ecologically centered cultures represent the majority of the world's population. Because they are not oriented toward creating new technologies and monetizing their knowledge and relationships, they are less visible than the promoters of Western development highlighted by the media and Western educational institutions. Thus, the efforts of Freire's critics are directed toward strengthening local traditions of knowledge that are being threatened by the spread of the Western-based monoculture. The promotion of universals, whether in the form of representing critical reflection as the only valid approach to knowledge, the Western ideal of the autonomous individual, or the economic assumptions underlying the World Trade Organization, represents an effort to sustain a tradition of exploitation that current changes in the Earth's ecosystems are forcing us to abandon. The environment will also force us to recognize that the future lies with the revitalization of local knowledge and cultures that are as diverse as ecosystems. And it will force us to acknowledge that the industrial model of progress and the deep cultural assumptions that it is based on (and which Freirean thinkers share) is the reactionary position today.

The personal background of the conference participants, as well as the other contributors to this volume, reflects another change as basic as the emerging scientific consensus on global warming. The experience of living in the cultures they were originally attempting to transform through a Freirean approach to combining literacy with a critical and thus more politicized consciousness made them aware that the regeneration of vernacular traditions, which had been refined over generations of learning about the limits and possibilities of their bioregions, should be the primary basis for resisting colonization. Resistance, in effect, was in continuing the traditions of local knowledge and mutual aid that contributed to the self-sufficiency of the community. As the title of several of the chapters in this volume suggest, the real question becomes: Who are the oppressed—the Freirean agents of emancipation or the people who were to be emancipated from the intergenerational knowledge that is the basis of their identity and culture? This self-reflection involved a complexity of thinking that recognized that beneath the surface of oppressive conditions (often the result of earlier colonizing policies) that needed to be addressed was a reservoir of community-sustaining local knowledge. In effect, the papers presented at the Freire and Beyond Conference represent an effort to bring the assessment of Freire's ideas into the broader discourse of anticolonial thinking found in such books as Wolfgang Sachs' *The Development Dictionary* (1992) and *Global Ecology* (1993), Frédérique Apffel-Marglin and Stephen Marglin's *Dominating Knowledges* (1990), Vandana Shiva's *Monocultures of the Mind* (1993), Gustovo Esteva and Madhu Suri Prakash's *Grassroots Post-Modernism* (1998), and Frédérique Apffel-Marglin's (edited with PRATEC) *The Spirit of Regeneration: Andean Culture Against Western Notions of Development* (1998).

The growing resistance within Third World cultures to the Western model of development is being expressed in a number of ways that highlight the growing convergence between Third World activists and environmentalists. Both groups recognize that traditions of economic self-sufficiency (which include cooperative associations, local markets, and local systems of exchange) have a smaller impact on local ecosystems. They also recognize that the revitalization of intergenerational knowledge is important to limiting the monetization of the commons, which are coming under increasing pressure from multinational corporations to open up new markets and to gain further access to natural resources. Both Third World activists and environmentalists also recognize the importance of maintaining linguistic and thus epistemic diversity. As languages encode a culture's

way of understanding relationships and the attributes of the participants in both the human and natural communities, maintaining the
diversity of languages is essential to preserving the renewable characteristics of local ecosystems. It is noteworthy that the conference
participants were especially clear about the inability of Freire and
his current interpreters to recognize that critical reflection, although
appropriate in certain contexts, is only one of many valid approaches
to knowledge. They understood that critical reflection, depending on
context, could undermine forms of knowledge and systems of moral
reciprocity essential to living within the limits of natural systems. To
make the point more directly, the conference participants were able
to clarify the double bind inherent in promoting a universal vision
of human nature and mode of inquiry in the current context where
linguistic and species extinctions are increasingly intertwined.

Missing at the conference, and in the chapters in this book, was
a genuine dialogue with the leading educational theorists who are
promoting Freire's ideas in the nation's colleges of education. At
first glance it would appear that the proponents of indigenous self-
determination could be challenged by the Enlightenment-oriented
thinking of Freire's current promoters. To Western thinkers, the
Freirean vocabulary, which includes such terms as *oppression, critical
consciousness, democracy, dialogue,* and *revolutionary praxis,* appears as
especially suited to analyzing the linkages between the many forms
of injustice being perpetuated by social elites and by economic and
political systems that remain unresponsive to the impoverishment
that can be laid at their doorsteps.

The irony is that the colonizing natures of Christianity and the
Industrial Revolution (which is now in its digital phase of development) were also based on the idea that the individual needs to be
emancipated from the backwardness of non-Western traditions.
Christian missionaries viewed emancipation as necessary if individuals were to recognize the connections between their present moral
agency and future salvation. The Industrial Revolution also required
that individuals be emancipated from the web of intergenerational
responsibilities and support systems—otherwise they would be less
reliable as consumers and factory workers. These emancipatory
efforts were justified in a vocabulary strikingly similar to that used

by Freire and his followers. For example, "progress," "freedom," and "individualism" were key metaphors in the thinking of classical liberals who provided the conceptual foundations for the Industrial Revolution, in the thinking of Christian missionaries who promoted literacy as the key to unlocking the chains of oppressed thinking, and in the thinking of Freire and his present interpreters. The dialogue between those who are now questioning Freire's Western assumptions and the educational theorists who are turning critical reflection into a mantra in colleges of education also could have focused on how scientific and technological elites rely on critical reflection as their primary mode of inquiry—and the role these groups play in the current rush to globalize Western technological dependencies.

Freire is often represented by his followers as originating the idea that the primary task of the teacher should be to foster critical reflection. However, the reality is that critical reflection has been promoted by Western philosophers since the time of Socrates. Critical reflection has been used for varied purposes—from deconstructing the systemic roots of oppression to advancing technologies that have had the unanticipated consequence of undermining community and contaminating the environment. What seems to be common to everyone who promotes critical reflection is that they repeat the mistake made by earlier Western philosophers. That is, they fail to recognize the profound difference in cultural ways of knowing. In arguing that critical reflection is the *only* means of acquiring empowering knowledge, they turn a mode of knowing that is highly useful (indeed, indispensable) in certain contexts into a source of disempowerment—and even cultural domination. The contributors to this volume have made this limitation in Freire's thinking a primary focus of their analyses.

Although recognizing the good intentions of Freire, and that the use of his pedagogy might be useful in contexts where people already share his Western assumptions, the consensus among the postcolonial thinkers in this book is that the ecological crisis and the growing refusal of indigenous cultures to view themselves as subjects require a new conceptual and moral basis for educational reform. Reforms based on Western assumptions perpetuate the double bind of using the same mind-set to solve problems that it created in the first place.

This double bind can only be avoided by ensuring that decolonizing educational reforms must be grounded in a knowledge of and a respect for local cultural traditions. In light of the growing ecological crisis, the intergenerational traditions that strengthen community patterns of mutual support and reduce reliance on consumerism must be given special attention. The diversity of languages spoken today suggests the diversity of cultural ways of knowing and thus the diversity of approaches to educational reform that must be taken. Asking the following questions will help avoid framing educational reforms in ways that continue the process of subjugating indigenous cultures to the requirements of a Western-style (and environmentally destructive) global economy: What are the ways in which different cultures pass on and renew their understanding of moral reciprocity within their communities and between humans and the other forms of life in their bioregion? What traditions enable communities to keep market-oriented activities in balance with other aspects of community life and not, as is the current situation in Western cultures, in a state of continual expansion? What are the ways in which a collective awareness of the sacred is renewed over generations? What aspects of Western ways of knowing can be adapted to local use without fostering new dependencies? What understandings are needed in order to democratize, within the context of the indigenous culture, the impact of Western science, technology, and deep cultural assumptions? The answers to these questions, and the way they are translated into educational reforms, must come from within the local culture. They cannot be imposed by educational theorists located in elite Western colleges of education, or by educational theorists who appear to be members of the indigenous culture but are, by virtue of their Western education, agents of Westernization.

The problem of reforming colleges of education in Western countries, especially in North America, is daunting in other ways. As pointed out elsewhere in this volume, Freire's pedagogy is based on cultural assumptions that are the basis of a wide range of progressive educational reforms—from constructivist theories of how students create their own ideas to the increasingly widespread use of computers in the classroom. Marginalized cultural groups in North America still possess distinctive though increasingly attenuated traditions that provide vital reference points for guiding educational reforms in ways that renew their patterns of community and intergenerational connectedness. The special challenge facing these groups is determining how to renew their own traditions while at the same time providing for the realization of individual needs and aspirations within the dominant culture.

As members of minority cultures are poorly represented in faculties of education, the problem of conceptualizing alternatives to the wide range of "progressive" (i.e., read hegemonic and ecologically indifferent) educational reforms is even more complex. This is partly because these culturally mainstream professors of education are not grounded in alternative cultural ways of knowing and community traditions. A major reason radical reforms that address the cultural roots of the ecological crisis will be difficult to achieve is that this group, along with the classroom teachers and educational bureaucrats that have passed through their classrooms, control the direction of educational reform. Articulating an alternative to the dominant paradigm, which Freire and his followers share with other progressive educators, will require extended clarifications of how an ecojustice-oriented curriculum addresses the ecological crisis while at the same time contributing to cultural diversity.

The chapters by the Third World activists should be viewed as a source of constructive criticisms of Freire and his followers—a constructive criticism that Freire himself called for during the last years of his life. That is, the essays by the Third World activists identify the silences and double binds that cannot be ignored in the same way that Western critics of critical pedagogy have been dismissed as reactionary thinkers. The silences and double binds include the failure to acknowledge other ways of knowing beyond that of critical reflection—and thus the diversity of knowledge systems of the world's cultures, the failure to recognize the intergenerational nature of the commons that represents the deep cultural basis for resisting turning daily life into market relationships, and the failure to recognize that generalizing their own taken-for-granted culturally specific assumptions is imperialistic (even when done in the name of emancipation). These criticisms are constructive if the followers of Freire interpret them as challenges to rethink what now separates their universal vision of social justice from the practice and theory of ecojustice that is being pursued in many Third World and Western cultures.

Freire warned against turning his ideas into a new dogma (which I refer to in my chapter), and he urged that a dialogue be undertaken with others who have a different basis for understanding the issues that need to be addressed. For a dialogue to become something more than the exchange of ideas with others who share the same deep cultural assumptions, it will be necessary for Freire's followers to address the issues raised by the women and men who attempted to utilize his ideas in different non-Western cultural contexts. These issues include:

1. *The need for a more balanced understanding of the role that intergenerational knowledge plays in sustaining the nonmonetized relationships and activities of community life.* This better sense of balance as well as deeper understanding of the complexity of intergenerational knowledge become, in different cultural contexts, the basis of community dialogue about what needs to be intergenerationally renewed and what needs to be reformed.

2. *The need for a more complex and supportive understanding of different cultural approaches to development—and of the deep cultural assumptions they are based on* (which does not always mean acceptance of how they treat their marginalized groups). Many Third World cultures, as well as minority cultures in the West, represent alternatives to the mainstream neoliberal model of development, with its emphasis on creating greater dependence on Western technology and consumerism. Many of these cultures represent the daily practice of resistance, as opposed to seemingly endless reiterations of abstract theories of resistance.

3. *The need for an understanding of the teacher as a mediator between local culture and the culture now being globalized.* As pointed out in the chapters in this volume, the teacher-as-emancipator too often alienates students from the intergenerational knowledge of their own culture while at the same time converting them (to use a good missionary term) to the Western patterns of thinking that will leave them with the romanticized idea that they are self-directing individuals—

an idea that fails to protect them from the impoverishment that too often accompanies a monetized economy. As a cultural mediator, the teacher needs to cooperate with the local community in valorizing its different ways of encoding and renewing knowledge that contribute to moral reciprocity and mutual support while at the same time helping students to understand the gains and too-often-hidden losses connected with Western systems of knowledge and technology.

4. *The need for a more critical understanding of the liberal assumptions that underlie various constructivist approaches to education (including critical pedagogy), and how these assumptions are also shared by current advocates of globalization.* As I point out in the Afterword, assumptions about the progressive nature of change, a human-centered universe, individualism as the source of intelligence and moral judgments, and the use of evolution to explain the developments of culture (which both Dewey and Freire rely on) are basic to both the thinking of so-called "conservative" and emancipatory educational theorists—and to the thinking of politicians and CEOs who are promoting economic globalization.

It is only as the followers of Freire address these issues that they will be able to avoid the double bind that the Third World contributors to this book have brought into focus. Emancipating students and adults from their own cultural traditions of multiple community sources of knowledge and systems of interdependence, while at the same time colonizing them to adopt the overly simplistic view of critical reflection as the only true source of knowledge, brings out how Western godwords obfuscate one of the more problematic double binds promoted in Western universities. It is hoped that the deep sense of social justice that motivates Freire's many followers will lead them to recognize that the women and men who attempted to utilize Freire's ideas in non-Western cultural settings have identified the need for a more culturally grounded and ecologically informed approach to educational reform.

1

From a Pedagogy for Liberation to Liberation From Pedagogy

Gustavo Esteva
Dana L. Stuchul
Madhu Suri Prakash

Given the well-established image of Freire as a progressive, radical, or even revolutionary educator, it may seem preposterous, outrageous, or even ridiculous to present him—as we do in this chapter—as a conservative thinker and practitioner. Even more, on both theoretical and political grounds, we present him as a colonizer. This chapter explores how and why Freire's pedagogy for liberation is counterproductive, creating unintended corruption.

We believe that Freire was a man of integrity and profound social commitments. He was particularly committed to deep social transformation for liberating the "oppressed," as he called them. Yet, in spite of his intentions, we observe that he adopted assumptions or presuppositions that served the system he wanted to change. Instead of its transformation, his ideas nourished its conservation and reproduction.

THE CORRUPTION OF AWARENESS

During the 1960s, a new awareness emerged among sections of the educated elite across the world. Recognizing the very serious wrongs of their social, political, and environmental landscapes, they wanted change. Some, attempting to escape from the established world and its set of institutions and rules, marginalized themselves from this world. Others attempted to make, with their lives and livelihood, the changes they wanted for the world. Still others bore on their shoulders the responsibility to change the world. Freire was one of them. During these years, progressive intellectuals and activists also proffered in Latin America a radical critique of capitalism, to define the direction of the change they wanted and the desirable outcome for everyone. Many of them also shared the path defined by the *guerrilleros,* who reformulated the European tradition of the "enlightened vanguard." Instead of a party to develop the conscience/organization necessary for leading the people to their emancipation, they created the guerrilla.

Although inspired by Fidel Castro and Che Guevara, Freire searched for an alternative to guerrilla warfare and to the authoritarian state that he considered its usual outcome. Freire wanted the change to start with the people themselves, with their conscientization. Convinced that both oppressors and oppressed were dehumanized by oppression, he assumed that a new consciousness born of enlightened literacy would enable both to be fully human again and to eradicate the horrors of modern oppression. According to Freire, "The oppressors, who oppress, exploit and rape by virtue of their power, cannot find in this power the strength to liberate either the oppressed or themselves. Only power that springs from the weakness of the oppressed will be sufficiently strong to free both" (Freire, 1971, p. 32). But he also assumed that the oppressed cannot liberate themselves by themselves. They are submerged within oppression, in the world of the oppressor; they are dehumanized, divided, inauthentic beings. They need an outside critical intervention.

In theorizing this critical intervention, Freire's pedagogy grew. According to Freire, a pedagogy was needed to conceive and implement such intervention: a pedagogy of the oppressed. A group of liberated pedagogues, fully conscienticized in such pedagogy, would conceive and carry out educational projects with the oppressed in the process of organizing them. At first a pedagogy of the oppressed, this pedagogy would then become a pedagogy of all people in the process of permanent liberation, a pedagogy of humankind (Freire, 1971, p. 39). Freire's pedagogy is thus best understood as a pedagogy for mediators qua liberators. He did not address himself to the oppressed, who had lost their humanity. Freire wrote for critical educators, revolutionary leaders, social workers, organic intellectuals—a motley crowd of characters who in his view could and would dedicate themselves to the liberation of the oppressed. He attempted to teach them the moral and political virtues, as well as the technical tools, that would enable them, through their own liberation, to perform the function he ascribed to them. Substitutes for a revolutionary party or for guerrilla activities, the new enlightened vanguard could make possible the desirable change.

Freire believed, with Marx, that people are products of circumstances and upbringing, but also that people can change their circumstances. He thus departs from any mechanical, materialist determinism. But he does not explain why the only people who can change circumstances—and thus change other people and the world—are his privileged agents of change, the educators educated by him. And this is the point. There is no need to assume, like Berger (1974), that Freire's consciousness raising implies the arrogance of higher class individuals with respect to the lower class population. However, there is no doubt that Freire located himself in a tradition that implicitly or explicitly dismisses, suppresses, or disqualifies the abundant historical evidence of how people have rebelled by themselves against all sorts of oppressors. Freire's construction of mediators expresses a corruption of his awareness of oppression. His "conscience" operates as a veil, hiding from "liberated" agents of change their own oppression, the fact that their conscience is still embedded in an oppressive system and thus becomes counterproductive. Furthermore, it veils that such "conscience" adds oppression to the oppressed, disabling them while dismissing, denying, or disqualifying the fullness of their initiatives. This operation not only implies a specific, untenable arrogance—the hubris of possessing the true, universal conscience—it also serves the purpose of legitimizing the right of intervention in the lives of others.

In historical perspective, the operation, which transforms awareness into "conscience" and conscience into conscientization, is but another name for colonization, for the very process of establishing the oppression. As Illich (1982) observed, "Conscientization consists of the colonization and standardization of vernacular probity and honor through some 'catholic' (that is, universally human) set of institutional rules." It constitutes, for Illich, "a perversion of the original Christian idea of reform:"

> What has been called the "process of civilization" builds on a process that could be called "conscientization." The term has been coined in Brazil to label a kind of political self-help adult education organized mostly by clergymen popularizing Marxist categories to help the poor discover that they are "humans." I would call conscientization all professionally planned and administered rituals that have as their purpose the internalization of a religious or secular ideology. (pp. 158–159)

Conscientization is, in fact, new wine for old bottles—the bottles of colonization. During the last several centuries, all kinds of agents have pretended to "liberate" pagans, savages, natives, the oppressed, the underdeveloped, the uneducated, undereducated, and the illiterate in the name of the Cross, civilization (i.e., Westernization), capitalism or socialism, human rights, democracy, a universal ethic, progress, or any other banner of development. Every time the mediator conceptualizes the category or class of the oppressed in his or her own terms, with his or her own ideology, he or she is morally obligated to evangelize: to promote among them, for their own good, the kind of transformation he or she defines as liberation. Yet, a specific blindness seems to be the common denominator among these mediators: They seem to be unaware of their own oppression. In presuming that they have succeeded in reaching an advanced level or stage of awareness, conscience, or even liberation (at least in theory, in imagination, in dreams) and even more, that what their oppressed lack is this specific notion or stage, they assume and legitimate their own role as liberators. Herein, they betray their intentions.

THE CORRUPTION OF LOVE

At the very end of his life, Freire (1997) wrote a short book, *Pedagogy of Freedom*. In it, he offers a meditation on his life and work, while returning to his most important themes. Freire reminds us that his education, his pedagogy, are pointedly and purposively ideological and interventionist. It requires mediators. Here again, it addresses those mediators: a final call to involve them in the crusade. The leitmotiv of the book, the thread woven through every page as it occurred every day in the life of Freire, is the affirmation of the universal ethic of the human being: universal love as an ontological vocation. He recognizes its historical character. Derived from *caritas*, the Greek and Latin word for love, charity—motivated by care, by benevolence, by love for the other—is essential to the vocation of each person. But Freire also implores us that the universal ethic of the human being is specifically the ethic of human solidarity. He proclaims solidarity as a historical commitment of men and women, in order to promote and instill the universal ethic of universal love of human beings (Freire, 1997, p. 13). In this way, solidarity legitimizes intervention in the lives of others in order to conscienticize them. And *caritas* softens the universal, ethical imperative of conscientization. If "conscience" means in this context a form of human guidance and arbitration that has been internalized, "conscientization" is the process by which those endowed with such conscience are compelled to universalize it, to bring it to every one. If such conscience implies a corruption of awareness, as we contend, the process of conscientization implies something worse: a corruption of love.

Freire was fully aware of the nature of modern aid, of what he called false generosity. He identified clearly the disabling and damaging impact of all kinds of such aid. Yet, for all of his clarity and awareness, he is unable to focus his critique on service, particularly that service provided by service professionals. Freire's specific blindness is an inability to identify the false premises, presuppositions, and dubious interventions—in the name of care—of one specific class of service professionals: educators. In its modern institutional form, qua service, care is the mask of love. This mask is not a false face. The modernized service providers believe in their care and love, perhaps more than even the serviced. The mask is the face (McKnight, 1977, p. 73). Yet, the mask of care and love obscures the economic nature of service, the economic interests behind it. Even worse, this mask hides the disabling nature of service professions, like education.

All of the caring, service professions are presented as a "cure" for a deficiency, lack, or need that the professional service can best satisfy. Modern living has now become so dependent on such services that it is rarely perceived how they have transformed traditional sufficiency into the need they supposedly satisfy. Modern needs are not born out of necessities, as human limitations are defined in traditional societies. Modern needs are created through forms of deprivation and destitution, which reorganize the society and redefine the human condition. The "needy man," a new species, is a product of capitalism and is continually reproduced in the economic society.

Those arriving destitute in the cities of England in the 16th century needed employment for the first time in their lives . . . and in history. The enclosure of their commons, where they were able to fulfill all of their necessities for centuries, had transmogrified their condition. They could no longer live by their means and ways. For their sustenance, they now needed employment. The process continued, all over the world, creating not only generation after generation of jobless people but also all other modern needs. When learning, for example, was redefined as education and the traditional freedom and capacity for learning in commons was ruled out or severely restricted, millions of people were transmogrified into the uneducated or undereducated, desperately in need of educational services, always scarce and insufficient for the majority.

Freire applied the logic behind the construction of modern needs to the conscience he conceived. In attributing such need to his oppressed, he also constructed the process to satisfy it: conscientization. Thus, the process reifies the need and the outcome: Only conscientization can address the need for an improved conscience and consciousness, and only education can deliver conscientization. This educational servicing of the oppressed, however, is masked as care, love, vocation, historical commitment, as an expression of Freire's universal ethic of solidarity. Freire's blindness is his inability to perceive the disabling effect of his various activities or strategies of conscientization. He seems unaware that the business of modern society is service and that social service in modern society is business (McKnight, 1977, p. 69). Today, economic powers like the United States pride themselves in being postindustrial, with the replacement of smoke stacks and sweatshops moved to the South, with an economy retooled for global supremacy in providing service. The global economy creates and expands needs requiring service professionals, promising unlimited economic growth.

Freire was particularly unable to perceive the impact of the corruption that occurs when the oppressed are transformed into the objects of service as clients, beneficiaries, and customers. Having successfully created a radical separation between his oppressed and their educators, Freire was unsuccessful in bringing them together, despite all his attempts to do so through critical dialogue, deep literacy, and his other key concepts for empowerment and participation. All these pedagogical and curricular tools of education prove themselves repeatedly to be counterproductive: They produce the opposite of what they pretend to create. Instead of liberation, they add to the lives of oppressed clients more chains and more dependency on the pedagogy and curricula of the mediator.

RESISTING LOVE: THE CASE
AGAINST EDUCATION

Freire never questioned his central presupposition that education is a universal good, part and parcel of the human condition. In spite of the fact that he was personally exposed for a long time to an alternative view, he failed to critically examine his presuppositions. This seems to us at least strange, if not abhorrent.[1]

---

[1] Paulo Freire and Ivan Illich parted ways when Illich, in the 1970s, moved from the criticism of schooling to the criticism of what education does to a society; that is, from promoting alternatives *in* education to seeking alternatives *to* education.

Freire was explicitly interested in the oppressed. His entire life and work were presented as a vocation committed to assuming their views, their interests. Yet, he ignored the plain fact that for the oppressed, the social majorities of the world, education has become one of the most humiliating and disabling components of their oppression, perhaps even the very worst.

Education creates two classes of people everywhere: the educated and the uneducated or undereducated. The educated, a minority, receive all kinds of privileges from their position. The rest get all kinds of deprivation and destitution. No literacy campaign or educational project has or can overcome that deprivation and destitution in any society. Why did Freire close his eyes to such facts? Like all other educational reformers, he concentrated his efforts on polishing and cosmetizing people's chains. This further legitimized and deepened the oppression he was supposedly struggling against.

Despite the fact that the uneducated are not able to read the texts of the educated, they are not stupid.[2] They retain their common sense. In the era of accelerated educational reforms, the uneducated are better equipped to accept the fact denied by the educated: the foolishness of placing faith in the possibility of secular salvation through education. The growing awareness among the illiterate, the uneducated, and the undereducated that the enterprise of education will not "save" them or bring them security today marks the beginning of the end of the era of education.

For the experts, the contemporary state of education is dire. The educational system becomes more oppressive to those enrolled within it, even as it expands. With every step of its expansion, teaching becomes more mechanical, monotonous, and irrelevant. Students discover faster than their teachers can hide how irrelevant their learning is—how little it prepares them to do useful work or to live well a good life.

Despite this, reform proposals proliferate, grouped into three categories of reformers. Some look to improve the classroom: its methods, equipment, or personnel. Others attempt to liberate it

---

[2] In fact, the very idea of modern education emerged with the conviction, generalized in the 17th century, that men are born stupid. Stupidity became equivalent to original sin. Education became its cure, defined as the inverse of vital competence.

from any bureaucratic imposition, promoting teachers, parents, and communities as the principal decision makers for determining the content and methods of education. Still others attempt to transform the whole society into a classroom, with new technologies substituting for the closed space of the classroom, providing for open markets and remote teaching. The reformed, free, or worldwide classrooms represent three stages in the escalation of interventions to increase social control and to subjugate people. Educators continue to educate the world in the fallacy that education is as old as the hills. However, the idea of education is exclusively modern. Born with capitalism, education perpetuates it. The past is colonized every time the cultural practices or traditions for learning, study, or initiations into traditions of nonmodern peoples are reduced to that category called "education."

Across the globe, education is promoted in the name of equality and justice. Education is presented as the best remedy for the oppressive inequalities of modern society. It produces, however, exactly the opposite. Education creates the most oppressive of the class divisions now in existence today, separating people into two groups: the "knowledge capitalists" and the "destitute." In this new class structure, more value is attributed to those consuming more knowledge. And because society invests in them for the creation of "human capital," the means of production are reserved for them. The few receive all kinds of privileges, whereas the uncredentialed majority suffers all kinds of discriminations and disqualification.

Beyond any consideration of the quality of the services provided by educational institutions, the fact remains that everywhere the outcome is the same: to disqualify the social majorities. According to the educational experts of UNESCO, 60% of the children now entering into the first grade will never be able to reach the level considered obligatory in their countries. They will live forever with the handicap of a distinctly modern social category: the "dropout." Meanwhile, a small minority will get 20 or 30 years of schooling. The contemporary compulsion, now achieving epidemic proportions across the world, is to expand and to reform the educational system. This compulsion is derived from two well-established facts: (a) that more than two thirds of the people in the world are uneducated or undereducated, and (b) that increasingly, the educated can no longer find the types of jobs for which their education supposedly prepared them.

Unceasingly, educational reformers debate the content or method of their reform agendas while sharing the same purpose: the reaffirmation of the social prejudice that holds that education via schooling and its equivalents is the only legitimate way to prepare people to live, and that whatever is learned outside of them has no value. New generations are thus educated to consume knowledge under the assumption that their success will depend on the quantity and quality of their consumption of that commodity, and that learning about the world is better than learning from the world.

Today's most dangerous reformers are those who promote the substitution of the classroom for the massive distribution of knowledge packages via global communication technologies. These reformers go further in establishing knowledge consumption as a basic need for survival. While traditional reformers are still promising more and better schools, these current reformers are at this moment winning the race. They present themselves as the only ones who will be able to achieve the goal accepted by everyone: equality of access.[3] Rather than diminishing the need for classrooms, these reformers extend its function. Theirs is an attempt to transform the global village into an environmental womb in which pedagogic therapists will control, under the appearance of a free market, the complex placenta necessary for nourishing every human being. Furthermore, the regulation of intellectual rights, now being negotiated in international institutions, will serve to protect the corporations that produce and distribute the knowledge packages that from now on will define education in the global campus.

Like capital, education was initially promoted through force. Today, police and armies are still used to extend and deepen educational control. However, education has now been established as a personal and collective need. Like other needs, it has been transformed into a right. More than bureaucratic imposition, education

---

[3] The promise is, of course, another illusion, legitimizing the current campaign. Less than 1% of the people in southwest Asia have access to the Internet. Two thirds of the people on Earth have never made a phone call. So much for the equality of access through the Internet!

has become a legitimate and universally accepted social addiction: It stimulates knowledge consumers to freely, passionately, and compulsively acquire their chains and thus contribute to the construction of the global Big Brother. In attempting to define "education," Tolstoy observed that education is a conscious effort to transform someone into something. More and more, that "something" is a subsystem, a creature that functions within an oppressive system. As a central tool for reproducing this system, modern technologies, particularly those linking TV and the Internet, will lead the oppression farther than ever before.

Marx observed that the blind compulsion to produce too many useful things would end up producing too many useless people. The current global escalation of educational needs only accelerates the process. And, although capital has more appetite than ever, it has not enough stomach to digest everyone. The promise of employment for everyone is increasingly recognized as an illusion. Globalized markets simply cannot absorb the masses. Increasingly, people become disposable human beings: Capital cannot use or exploit them. However, by giving them, with public funds, access to knowledge packages, capital educates them as consumers and prepares them for the moment in which it can subsume them again in the system of exploitation.

LIBERATION FROM PEDAGOGY

These "disposable" people have started to react everywhere. Today, the proliferation of initiatives escaping the logic of capital is evident. Everywhere, "disposable" people are transforming the drama of exclusion into an opportunity to follow their own path and to create by themselves their own lives. One of their first steps is to escape education. In 1953, when education was included in the promotion of development launched by Truman in 1949, UNESCO experts concluded that the main obstacle to education in Latin America was the indifference or resistance of most parents. Eleven years later, the same experts warned that no Latin American society would be able to satisfy the demand for education. Their campaign had been more than successful. Educated to accept the idea of education, parents began to clamor for more teachers and schools, always in short supply for the majority. Throughout the world during different periods, the same process was reproduced. During the last 20 years, the impulse to claim or resist education, however, has been transformed into a struggle for liberation—liberation from professional pedagogy and the very idea of education.

The illusion that education delivers employment, prestige, and social mobility, which proved real for a minority, led many people to accept its high price: severe cultural destruction and dismembering of family and community life (Stuchul, 1999). Step by step, the social majorities received proof that diplomas did not certify competence or skills but the number of hours and years during which a student has sat on a chair in a classroom. Far from guaranteeing employment, they doom many of those advancing up the educational ladder to permanent frustration. The humiliation of engineers or lawyers, forced to work as taxi drivers or hotel porters, has become an opportunity for liberation for those without diplomas or those having one of low value. In time, the "disposables" or the educated unemployed/unemployable are revaluing their own traditional wisdom, skills, and competencies for living.

While the Internet accelerates the irrelevance of most schooling, the social majorities are bypassing schooling altogether as they do, whenever they can, with all bureaucratic impositions and the addictions of the rich. They are no longer surrendering themselves to the illusions of education. People are saying, "Enough!" while recovering, little by little, their traditional arts of learning. In rejecting the need of mediators and the dominant paradigm that holds that the people cannot govern themselves or change and rebel by themselves autonomously, we are of course affirming the opposite: that the people can govern themselves. Even more, it is our contention that people liberate themselves from oppressors only when both the initiative and the struggle come from them—from within themselves rather than from external agents of change. Instead of pro-motion (which operates under the assumption that the people are paralyzed or are moving in the wrong direction), those taking initiatives at the grass roots to govern themselves autonomously or democratically speak of co-motion: moving with the people, rather than moving the people.

In Spanish, the words *conmover* and *conmoción* are instructive and strong in their denotation. *Conmoción* means not only to dance with the other the common tune (which does not necessarily define a common conscience), it also denotes moving together with the heart and the stomach, not only with the brain, with rationality. The real plurality of the world is thus manifest in a pluralist attitude, fully respecting both the radical otherness of the other and his or her visions and initiatives. Co-motion may thus operate as a vaccine against the corruption of awareness and love.

In response to colonization, Dion-Buffalo and Mohawk recently suggested that colonized peoples have three choices: (a) to become good subjects, accepting the premises of the modern West without much question, (b) to become bad subjects, always resisting the parameters of the colonizing world, or (c) to become nonsubjects, acting and thinking in ways far removed from those of the modern West (quoted in Esteva & Prakash, 1998, p. 45). The assumption of Freire is that his oppressed are trapped within the dominant ideology, that they have been dehumanized by the system, that they are its subjects. But his rebellion, as much as his solidarity, succeeds at best in creating the condition of a bad subject, a rebel subject. In this way, neither Freire nor his conscienticizers can perceive their own oppression. As the old Arab saying wisely warns: "Choose your enemy well; you will become like him." Freire's presuppositions trap him within the ideology of his oppressor. He becomes a bad subject, though not embracing his oppression, not loving his chains, or even loving power. Although bad, he remains yet a subject. By reducing his definition of himself, of his own being, to the terms of the oppressor, even for the sake of resisting or opposing him, he cannot become a nonsubject.

The initiatives happening among people at the grass roots in the era of globalization have solid and numerous historical precedents in what Shanin (1983) calls "vernacular revolutions." The term *vernacular* means native, indigenous, not of foreign origin or of learned formation (OED). The antonyms of vernacular are: cosmopolitan and worldly-wise, artificial and subtle, expert, official, universal, and scientific. When in the 19th century the idea of progress was accepted as self-evident, the dual conceptions of vernacular and its antonyms turned into the stages of a "necessary evolutionist scheme: the uplifting of men from the vernacular to the universal, the scientific and the sublime" (Shanin, 1983, p. 249). Changes made during the 20th century further transformed the meaning of vernacular:

> Now, vernacular was defined as unique, hand-made, informal, autonomous, self-generated or even native. . . . It is therefore a product or a situation in which the mass market, price accounting and bureaucratic administration cannot be handled to full effect. The directionality of progress becomes an official strategy of reforms due to bulldoze, replace in plastic and electronics or else to educate-out any vernacular substances, i.e. the inadequate and archaic products, humans and ways. (Shanin, 1983, p. 249)

According to the dominant modern perception, vernacular initiatives and movements, expressing the rebellion of the oppressed against their oppressors or at least their resistance, are unseen, irrelevant, or nonexistent. Or, even worse, they are viewed as counterproductive, traditionalist, parochial, fundamentalist, and reactionary or counterrevolutionary because they do not follow the official program. According to the prevailing perspective, the only movements or initiatives taken into account are those conceived and promoted by cosmopolitan, universal, educated agents of change, agents who educate the people toward progress, pointing the way out of the vernacular toward the universal . . . the global.

Yet, recent decades have increasingly revealed that the vision of a world integrated under the rule of reason, welfare, and the very ideal of progress has become archaic, an intellectual and conceptual artifact fit for any museum (Sachs, 1992; Sbert, 1992). No longer can the existence of vernacular revolutions be denied. Those studying the vernacular insurrections of subordinated knowledge with a new gaze have escaped the dominant dilemma: If your vision of the world is not associated with the idea of progress, you are going back in history. Instead, seeking considerations of social transformation in the full richness of peoples' cultural diversity, they are discovering the multiplicity, multidirectionality and multiquality of actual and potential social routes (Shanin, 1983, p. 250). What is therefore increasingly in question is the real nature and potential for transformation of the conscience, which all sorts of revolutionaries have attempted to instill in the people in order to promote their own projects. Berry (1972) states:

> The thinking of professional reformers and revolutionaries usually fails to escape the machine analogy operative in military and other coercive thinking. And a machine is by definition subservient to the will of only one man. In the formula Power to the People, I hear "Power to me, who am eager to run the show in the name of the People." The People, of course, are those designated by their benevolent servant-to-be, who knows so well what is good for them. Thus by diseased speech, politics, as usual, dispenses with the facts. (p. 41)

Often, when it becomes impossible to deny the very presence and the social and political impact of peoples' initiatives or vernacular revolutions, the dominant reaction is to associate them with prominent characters or charismatic leaders—of the likes of a Gandhi, Subcomandante Marcos, or Wendell Berry.[4] Such attributions of the origins and orientations of peoples' movements to enlightened or educated leaders legitimize the prejudice that nothing progressive can happen without mediators. It fails to recognize that teachers like Gandhi, Marcos, or Berry do not conscienticize, empower, or educate for liberation. Being the change they wish for the world, their

---

[4]A prominent case in point is the Zapatista movement. For the government, the political parties, many analysts, and even many of its followers and sympathizers, the Zapatistas are in fact reduced to the now famous Subcomandante Marcos. In this, they express their racist prejudice: The only educated White man of the movement, who has performed a brilliant role as speaker (a kind of cultural bridge between the indigenous peoples and the educated world), should be the one conceiving and leading the movement. Time and again, the Zapatistas have declared, or demonstrated with facts, that their uprising came from peoples' own initiative, from their communities, not from an enlightened leader. They affirm that they are not guerrillas: Instead of fish (the revolutionaries) that swim in the sea of the people, as Che Guevara said, they are the sea, the people themselves. They have no interest in seizing power. Even their army is subordinated to a civil command. Zapatismo was born from the communities themselves that have since then been in control. Marcos himself has explained how he was "converted" by the communities, which cured him of the ideological burden he brought to the jungle. But no fact seems to be able to dissolve the prejudice: The Zapatistas are still seen, by the elite, as a group of manipulated Indians under the control of a *mestizo*.

integrity, courage, and vitality cannot but be contagious. They boldly declare that the emperor is naked. He wears no clothes. He is not needed for the "good" of the people.

With their feet firmly on their soil, uneducated common men and women are recovering their own notions of learning and living free of educational mediation. Inasmuch as the noun *education* imposes a completely passive dependence on the system that provides education, people are substituting this noun with the verbs *to learn* and *to study*. Unlike the noun, these verbs reestablish the autonomous capacity for building creative relationships with others and with nature, relationships that generate knowing and wisdom. People are again acknowledging that to know is a personal experience, and that the only way to know, to widen the competencies for living, is to learn from the world, not about the world.

Everywhere, dissident groups are enjoying the sufficiency of their initiatives, the opening of new spaces for freedom (Prakash & Esteva, 1998). Here and there, some people close the schools or put them under community control. Instead of allocating public funds for education, they start public campaigns to impose heavy taxes on schooling, like those on alcohol and tobacco. Other campaigns seek to abrogate all laws making education obligatory. The main impulse of these initiatives, however, follows another direction. While the educated persist in their competitive struggle to consume more knowledge, the uneducated and undereducated are weaning themselves of the secular faith in such dependency. Confronted by the propaganda of knowledge peddling, they adopt the same attitude that they take before junk food: They know that the latter does not nourish, although sometimes it may curb hunger. They realize that education, akin to junk food, is unable to generate communal wisdom or to guide experience.

While Bill Gates and his colleagues prolong the agony of education, many people are anticipating its death with creative, convivial initiatives that widen their capacity for learning, studying, and for doing (instead of the capacity to buy and to consume), avoiding the various debilitations and dependencies fostered by education, however conceived. Such initiatives are proving useful in their living and working within their old or new commons. While undermining the dominant institutions, they prepare their inversion. Their hope: that the extinction of the ritual of schooling and of the myth of education is appearing on the horizon, a horizon that will represent the beginning of an era ending privilege and license (Illich, 1971; Stuchul, 1999).

Freire (1972) was entirely unable to anticipate such evolution or even to perceive the nature of the problem. In his very famous essay, "Education: Domestication or Liberation?", written 2 years after *Pedagogy of the Oppressed*, he presented the essence of his thesis: Education cannot be neutral.

> If we claim to go beyond the naive, formal interpretations of the human task of education, this must be the starting point of a critical dialectical reflection. Lacking this critical spirit, either because we are alienated to thinking statistically and not dynamically, or because we already have ideological interests, we are incapable of perceiving the true role of education, or if we perceive it, we disguise it. We tend to ignore or to obscure the role of education, which, in that it is a social "praxis," will always be at the service of the "domestication" of men or of their liberation. (p. 18)

From there on, Freire concentrated all his efforts, in that essay and in his life, on the idea of designing an "education for liberation." He was thus unable to perceive the victimization created by education and to derive the pertinent conclusions. He was unable to bring his brilliant critique of "banking education" to the modern enterprise called "education."

REFERENCES

Berger, P. L. (1974). *Pyramids of sacrifice: Political ethics and social change.* New York: Basic Books.
Berry, W. (1972). *A continuous harmony: Essays cultural and agricultural.* New York: Harcourt Jovanovich.
Esteva, G., & Prakash, M. S. (1998). *Grassroots postmodernism: Remaking the soil of cultures.* London: Zed Books.
Freire, P. (1971). *Pedagogy of the oppressed.* New York: Herder & Herder.
Freire, P. (1972). Education: Domestication or liberation. In *Prospects* (Vol. 2, No. 2, summer, pp. 15–24). Cambridge: Cambridge University Press.

Freire, P. (1997). *Pedagogy of freedom: Ethics, democracy, and civic courage.* Lanham, MD: Rowman & Littlefield.

Illich, I. (1971). *Deschooling society.* New York: Harper & Row.

Illich, I. (1982). *Gender.* New York: Pantheon.

McKnight, J. (1977). Professionalized service and disabling help. In I. Illich, I. K. Zola, J. McKnight, J. Caplan, and H. Shaiken, *Disabling professions* (pp. 63–74). London: Marion Boyars.

Prakash, M. S., & Esteva, G. (1998). *Escaping education: Living as learning within grassroots cultures.* New York: Peter Lang.

Sachs, W. (1992). One World. In W. Sachs (Ed.), *The development dictionary: A guide to knowledge as power* (pp. 102–115). London: Zed Books.

Sbert, J. M. (1992). Progress. In W. Sachs (Ed.), *The development dictionary: A guide to knowledge as power* (pp. 192–205). London: Zed Books.

Shanin, T. (1983). *Late Marx and the Russian road.* Berkeley, CA: University of California Press.

Stuchul, D. (1999). *Schooling as ritual and as technology: Explorations in the social thought of Ivan Illich.* Unpublished doctoral dissertation, The Pennsylvania State University, University Park, PA.

2

Nurturance in the Andes

Grimaldo Rengifo Vasquez

Where is the wisdom we have lost in knowledge?
Where is the knowledge we have lost in information?
—T. S. Elliot, Chorus I from *The Rock* (1934)

REGARDING FREIRE

Freire's blind spot was in not lending nature its due. Worried as we all were about achieving social justice, the Freirian pedagogic agenda was at first seen as developing the conceptual and methodological tools for the transformation of social relations that were at the very foundation of the social inequities. He neglected to reflect on the relations of domination by man over nature. Perhaps this neglect was in the very structure of our discourse. For modern man, nature is there to be transformed with a view to establishing the dominion of man over the Earth, not to converse with her. The dialogical discourse of emancipation was basically humanistic. The pedagogy of the oppressed was formulated as an instrument for the solution of social oppression, not for those concerned with the subjugation of nature, as if the solution to the ecological problem would emerge when humans stopped oppressing each other.

I remember that, in the summer of 1970, as a member of a literacy instruction team at the San Lorenzo irrigation project in Piura in the northern coast of Peru, I started my first classes with the so-called motivating phase. One of the plates that we presented depicted a mud house, typical in that rural area, in the process of being built. These plates were painted by students of the secondary school in which I taught or by teachers adept at painting. The idea was to represent with details a local reality that was part of the daily life of the people who attended, mostly small tenants and agricultural workers of cotton-growing haciendas. This plate would help us, by its familiarity, to rapidly initiate the dialogue with the peasants.

The "cultural circles" were composed of about 10 peasants, mainly male, and the dialogues started after dinner, around 8:00 in the evening. As electricity had not yet arrived in the area, we used kerosene lamps that lighted the plate around which we sat to talk in the penumbra. The methodological script followed the steps of every process of knowledge acquisition: to see, to judge, and to act. The first step was to *see* a reality happening outside the subject, who proceeds to its decomposition into parts. This section of the script implied that the peasants would abstract reality, which involved the active processing of sensorial, motor, and cognitive activities with the aim of obtaining a representation of that reality.

To *judge* that reality was the second step. At that moment, the contrast of peasant reality with that of the hacienda owners and the rich tenants of the time was attempted. The peasants were asked to compare their situations in terms of health, education, working conditions, and so forth, with those of the hacienda owners and other privileged segments of society. The dimensions of injustice and oppression had to be perceived and grafted in the consciousness of the peasants. The third part of the script was to *act* on that reality to propitiate its transformation. This was the political part of the literacy process because it implied the organization and mobilization of the peasants to modify the situation of the oppressed. In June of 1969, an agrarian reform conducted by the Peruvian military regime was initiated. The zone was no exception, and the large estates were declared as potentially affected by the government. It was in that political context that our alphabetization experience was developed.

Following this script, the first step of the educational action was to ask the participants what they saw in the plate; that is, to proceed to deconstruct it into its parts. (The first plate showed men working, a pile of mud, adobes, trees, hens, dogs, etc.) To achieve this, the leader of the circle called the attention of all participants to the particular situations in order to go beyond the global and familiar perception the peasants had of the plate at the beginning of the session. If the plate was well made, the peasants could even distinguish the persons depicted and the part of town where the house was being built and even the type of straw with which the mud was being mixed to make the blocks. The plate was not a representation for them. It was another way of presenting their life, and they established a very strong attachment to it. The leader of the circle then had to introduce them to the process of abstraction—to mentally separate, in pieces, the reality that peasants lived without any separation or seams, that is, holistically.

This process of disembedment of their daily experience in order to transform it into an object of analysis was, perhaps, the most complicated part of the alphabetization activity because it had to end in a representation of reality in the peasants' minds. It was a process the peasants resisted because it implied a mental effort that they were not used to. A way of reaching it—the represented reality—was to give different names to things. Thus, the thing *earth* became the object *nature* because it was there, as part of natural life. Meanwhile, *adobe* was the object *culture* because it had been made by man in his work of transformation starting from material lying in nature. Thus, when the leader pointed to adobe in the plate, the peasants would not say the name of the thing (adobe) but that of the concept (culture). This process was repeated over again until the reality objectified and represented could be distinguished in the peasants' mind through the concept. This initial dynamic ended with the assertion—made by the peasants—that they were cultured men because they made culture, as an attribute of their human nature is to transform nature by transforming themselves. We do not know if the peasants repeated the phrase out of their own comprehension or due to the ordinary meaning of the word *cultured* in the rural area then. The word cultured served to qualify, in the same way that uncultured was used to disqualify, a person.

But aside from these remarks, we were enthusiastic when the peasants repeated the phrase "peasants are cultured men." The phrase had the effect of placing on an even footing any man beyond his socioeconomic status, and certainly that hierarchical and subordinated relation between the peasants and the landowners was altered, thus giving place to a situation of peasant self-esteem. This was for us a basic precondition to judge the social situation and to facilitate its transformation, steps which were to continue during the whole process of alphabetization. It was then the moment to proceed to judging reality, which consisted of contrasting the situation of the peasants with an image of what it should be, with an objective image, a utopia. The next step was to act in such a way that reality approached that utopia, that is, constructing what was called a "new world." This sequence was repeated over again both during the motivating phase and in the very process of alphabetization.

The dynamics of learning to read and write, which came after the motivating phase, implied the elaboration of a vocabulary integrated with words that could generate cognitive processes oriented to discovering a new perception of reality, that is, to provoke conscientization. The pedagogic research of the period was full of investigations regarding "leading" words, but there was very little regarding the cognitive world of the peasants. It was assumed that the mind was the same in all cultures and what changed was the contents. Our concern was focused on overcoming the so-called magic consciousness whose development was a precondition to judge the reality to be transformed. The affects, the feelings, and the emotions were considered contextual dimensions for learning, but not their central elements. The senses were the energetic segment of the cognitive action, organs for informing a mind that had to be educated to transform information into concepts. We paid no attention to telling phrases mentioned by peasants in the cultural circles such as, "Juana knows how to nurture hens because she's got a hand for them." Besides that, the cult of the death, the vigils for their dead ancestors that lasted a whole week at the cemetery, and the practice of local medicine so respectful of nature, were considered relics of a magical past to be eliminated. The method and our own convictions demanded it.

Thus, every time we initiated the evening dialogue, we reiterated the distinction between nature and culture because, in our judg-ment, there could be no development of the capacity to transform the world without the appearance of a world of objects outside of, and independent of, the subject. The peasant's filial relationship with nature had to be changed during the process of alphabetization. Nature was there as an object, not as a person nor as another subject of the educational activity. At the same time that all knowledge de-pending on the senses was devalued, the humanist notion that man is the ultimate end and that everything else is to be subordinated was affirmed.

Freire knew well that to proceed from awareness, of simple opin-ion—*doxa*—to critical knowledge—*logos*—implied the breakage of the umbilical cord linking man with nature, because experience— that direct, emotional, and sensorial relationship with the things of the world—limits the emergence of the consciousness of the world, precludes the presence of the "object" installed in the mind as repre-sentation. Lived experience annuls the critical, scrutinizing, gaze on the world because there is a sort of interpenetrability between man and world, a common participation of similar attributes, a sensuous and collective participation in the world. It would be years later be-fore we began to understand the role of the sensuous in learning and in general in the relationship with nature. But at that time only the emergence of the ego, of subjectivity, mattered for knowing the world from a critical stance. The alphabetization experience did not come to a conclusion. The state administration considered that the experi-ence was dangerous and expelled the alphabetization team from the zone. However, the peasants would later go beyond the bureaucratic limits of the agrarian reform and would initiate more fundamental reforms by the takeover of the landed estates.

How much of what we did contributed to the change in social relations? That we do not know. Probably a bit. We should not forget that the agrarian reform had been a peasant demand long delayed and preceeded any conscientization process. There remains for many of us a certain satisfaction in having made friends with the peasants and that, in spite of the mental boredom, the sessions meant they had not driven us out from their houses and that some of them could finally read and write their names. We wonder, however, whether any critical consciousness that we looked after so persistently had finally taken root in their minds. I now believe that saying and writing the words that we demanded has not led them to represent the world but to nominate it. When they were asked to "take distance" from the plate, the peasants had difficulty in doing so because they felt themselves in the plate. This was not a representation of reality but reality itself. And when they were asked to speak on what the plate expressed, the speech referred to situations and circumstances of their lives without a structured, analytic, discursive language emerging in it. For many of them, the experience of the peasant struggles, which they had carried out for the recovery of their lands, had taught them that it was not necessary to objectify the land as a prerequisite for liberating it. They did not feel that Pachamama (the deity of regeneration of life) had to be transformed into a resource, into soil, that could then be measured and quantified. They have shown in history that they can at the same time integrate long-term revolutions without abandoning their rituals and their filial relationship with nature. Moreover, each participation in political struggles has been inspired by rituals and is done in conversation with the deities. They do not see any reason for breaking their links of familiarity with nature and deities in order to learn to read and write. For them, the diversity of knowledge is not lived as a substitution or imposition of one over the other but as enrichment. Paraphrasing T. S. Elliot, it could be said that knowledge does not make them lose their wisdom.

Among the peasants who make rituals to Mother Earth in the Andes, there are those who can read and write. Many of them are professionals also. School, even if it erodes embodied knowledge, does not substitute it with a rational relationship with nature. Life in the commons, not schooled learning, is associated with knowing how, knowing with the senses—an embodied rather than an abstracted knowledge. It is not the knowledge of *homo faber*, the Maker who creates the world out of nothing. It is a knowledge that recreates and regenerates the perennial world in which emotions and senses are not lived only as informers of a mind but also as possessors of knowledge. The hand knows because it is corporal; the body summarizes, if the expression is allowed, the biological and the psychological. Everything is expressed through it as a unit. The body perceives and speaks of the perceived, as the mind and the body are indissolubly united.

Years later I visited those villages where I began as a member of the alphabetization team and witnessed the participation of my former pupils in long peregrinations to sacred places, like the one that leads to the Captive Lord of Ayabaca. The ALFIN (Integral Alphabetization) program developed by the military government in the 1970s had not achieved the modification of the peasant magical mentality by applying the Freirian methodology. The ceremonies to the protecting mountains have continued and are now stronger, even in Lima, a capital with eight million inhabitants, where the Andean rituals have invaded spaces reserved for Christian celebrations.

In what follows, I reflect briefly on the attributes of the peasant mode of knowledge, an activity that I share with my friends at PRATEC and numerous groups of cultural affirmation who carry out activities accompanying the regeneration of peasant agriculture in diverse places in the Peruvian Andes. The consensus we have reached is that an approach centered on nurturance dissolves the problem left by Freire's humanism as it incorporates nature and the sacred into the regeneration of life.

NURTURANCE

The pedagogy of the oppressed, by placing the emphasis on the mind and by subordinating the sensuous and the affective to the cognitive, focuses on human beings in and by themselves. The capacity of reasoning and of perceiving the world locates the truth of things in the subject, so that truth is not the fit of mind to the thing, but the fit of the thing—become object—to the mind. The teacher, in this context, is the one who orients the minds of the pupils, whatever the method, in the search for truth. The nature of the human in the Andes is to be "in relation." Conversation, dialogue, participation, communal life are constitutive of it and not the isolation of each being. Community, the collective, is not external, but is the basis of existence. By associating with others, the community itself is what links everyone and everything so that what matters is the collective harmony that is found in the life of the entire community and not each of the "forms in themselves"—and least of all in the mental capacity of the individual that is given a privileged status in the West. This capacity, in Andean life, is never all by itself, but closely related, linked with the senses and all the living community that nests in each being.

To understand the emphasis on relation, we must first clarify what is meant by the idea of man from an Andean perspective. From the Western viewpoint, man—the human being—is an animal bearer of the idea, of reason, of spirit. That is what defines and what distinguishes him from other beings in nature. In the Quechua language, man is translated as *runa*. This is the common definition. The question is whether *runa* is also an animal bearer of the logos. In the Andes the families talk about the *anima* (soul), as something that inhabits every being in the world, be it human, plant, animal, stone, or lagoon. This *anima* is, in the lived experience of these families, a being that nests in each person. It is not something living intimately in community, in pair. The couple is more than the sum of two units; pair is what links, joins—the web that joins and connects the life of those who live in a pair. In the couple, the emphasis is on the moving web of life and not in each point and knot by itself.

In the festival honoring the first fruits of the land during the carnival season in Puno, the Aymara families celebrate ritually and joyfully. On the central day of the festivities, the potato tubers are called *Ispallas*—deities of the potato—not potatoes. For outsiders, such denomination can be considered an expression of the symbolization of an external deity incarnated in the potato, but this does not seem to be experienced in such a way by these families. Each being is experienced in certain circumstances as a deity too, so that it is potato and *Ispalla* at the same time; that is, nature and deity. Moreover, the women who participate in these festivities also do it in their condition as deities of the potato and are so considered, whereas the men are deities of the grains (*muchus* in Aymara). On that occasion and in such festive circumstances, one is either *Ispalla* or *muchu;* in other words, the deity nesting in each human being emerges. No one experiences this as a representation, a transformation, or a mutation. For the Andean families, the community is not external, but each being is a community in itself. Hence, the Aymara women speak about "their bodies" in plural referring to their own person.

Thus each person is a community of relations, the emphasis of an activity being not so much in each individual but in the conversation that individual maintains among its selves and with the rest of beings. This internal harmony is expressed through the senses, the feelings, and the emotions. It is a relation focused on affection. When a *runa* or *jaq'e* (human being in Aymara) is a mature person, what in the city is recognized as a person "of reason"—which means not so much that he or she is calculating but rather is reasonable—in the Aymara world he is called *chuyman jaq'e. Chuyma* in one of its meanings is the lung, the entrails. But it can also be understood as that which is inside, as the affective, the sentimental, the harmonizing part, the feelings. A *chuyman jaq'e* is a human being with heart, with feelings, a serene and quiet being, a harmonizer and capable of appeasing the hate, the passions, the envy, and every feeling or emotion that can weaken the health and the conversation between the community nesting in each one and the communities inhabiting the others, which transcends it, a metaphysical being, but a patent being, visible to eyes and the rest of the senses of these families, and makes a couple with the body in a symbiosis and harmonious mutuality that is crucial for the maintenance of life. If the *anima* leaves the body—as it is said—the body declines and can even die as such. The families, and in general the local healers, know when a corporeal disharmony is provoked by the absence of the *anima.* There exists a series of rituals to propitiate the return of the *anima* to the body that nests it, so that the couple body-mind recovers its harmony, its impulse, its will to live, its relation of symbiosis. The *runa,* in this context, is more than body, even when this entity expresses wholly and without separation between the psychological and the biological. It may be said that the runa expresses the feeling of life.

In this sense, the emphasis is placed not so much in each person, not even in her or his mind, but in the relation of empathy propitiated by the communal action, both pleasing and enriching. This being together not only refers to the association between humans; it is also related to doing things in conjunction with nature and the deities. Thus, doing together is a ceremony with intense ritual moments. The Andean expression denominating the weaving of the relations between the beings inhabiting the community is *nurturance.* Nurturance is the link, the knot that connects and ties each of the beings that populate the communal web. Nurturing is in Quechua *uyway,* and *uywa* is the nurtured. Nurturing is caring, cultivating, protecting, nestling, helping, assisting, feeding, breast-feeding, sustaining, maintaining, endearing, giving affection, conversing, singing, lulling. Nurturing in the sense of the word *uywa* is not an action originating in an active subject and going to another passive subject. Nor is it experienced as a hierarchical relation. It is a conversation, affective and reciprocal between equivalents.

In the Andes it is commonly heard that peasant women say, "As I nurture this potato, she nurtures me." The potato is not only nurtured but is also experienced as a nurturer of the humans herself. This manner of speaking dissolves the hierarchical relationship between humans and nature so rooted in modern Western culture in which nature is at the service of man. As everyone nurtures, nurturance is a relation of mutual service and conversation. When nurturing, I am nurtured myself. The relationship thus becomes an encounter between nurturers to regenerate life in an affective empathy that promotes the emergence of mutual affection. The harmony attained when a maize field flowers expresses the symbiosis that arises in the whole encounter between nurturers, be they humans, Pachamama, or waters. It is a perennial harmony that is integral to every circumstance. Thus there is no pretension of harmony for all time and place. Another moment will demand new forms of conversation and empathy with the signs that life gives, and there will arise the harmony corresponding to that moment.

As the Andean world is not composed of objects but of persons who converse, who nurture while being nurtured, their members are not interested in "knowing" the others because their world is not populated by objects to be known and transformed. The concern is placed in the mutual empathy, in perceiving the flavors, in receiving affectionately the conversing signs of the rest, because in the measure that the mutual conversation arises, the nurturing proceeds. Conversation does not end in an action that is the responsibility of someone to be changed, but in mutual nurturing. Hence, Andean conversation is seminal, regenerative, a dialogue to live and not to search for truth.

However, nurturance, like everything else in life, is not given, but it is learned. It is learned in conversation with others, in attentive listening, in the participation in activities, festivals, and rituals. Only he who listens, he who puts himself in the other, he who knows how to tune himself to the others, he who lets himself be nurtured, he who lives in completeness thoroughly, learns. In a diverse and changing world, learning has the peculiarity of being circumstantial and leads to a knowledge or nurturance valid only for that circumstance. Learning to harvest is learned in harvesting and it is valid for that harvest. If the moon indicates that it is time to sow, sowing has to be done. Recovering land cannot be done at any time. It has to be done when the lands ask so. Every activity has to be undertaken in its moment and carried out in the best of moods. Music that is sung must accompany nature, it must not disturb her. Music for sowing must be played and danced in sowing and not in harvest time. The place for nurturing is the *chacra*. A common definition of chacra refers to it as the place destined to the nurturance of plants and animals. The Aymara in southern Peru refer to the llama as *kayuni yapu*, chacra with feet. The chacra in this case refers to the animal. In other cases, a salt or gold mine is also called salt chacra or gold chacra. A grove can also be a chacra.

Wild potato is called in Quechua *atoq papa*, that is, potato cultivated by the fox. Similar names are also given to wild ocas or mashuas. Some wild grains are cultivated by the birds. The vicuña, a wild camelid of the Andes, is considered as nurturance of the mountain protector. Thus chacra in the Andes are not only cultivated by members of the human community but also by nature and the deities. In the Andean cosmovision, all those who inhabit it are chacareros (chacra makers). Chacra in this sense is a polisemic word: It refers to a place, but it is more than that. It also refers to a medium that generates life, where I nurture and am nurtured.

The concern of a nurturer does not limit itself to her chacra, that is the human chacra, but extends to the nurturance of the chacra of all the members of nature and of the deities. A chacra will be healthy to the extent in which all the chacras in the landscape are vigorous. Thus the health of the human collectivity is associated with the health of its chacras and to the whole of nature. Ritual ceremonies are conversations for the health of all these collectivities as the harmony of any of them is in relation with the harmony of the whole. Nurturance can be a contribution to a different pedagogy if the educational activity becomes the caring and careful accompaniment to a mode of relating to the world in which the emphasis is not placed in the beings themselves—humans and nature—but in the relation existing between them in the action of nurturing and being nurtured and in which the accompanist-teacher is part of the nurturing activity.

NURTURANCE OF THE SCHOOL

As just observed, despite the boredom that the peasants feel with the conscientization dynamic, it does not cause them to reject the possibility of learning to read, write, and to do mathematics. Moreover, school is already part of the peasant landscape. There is no community in which the school is absent. In what follows, we explore the relationship between community and school. As is well known, the school is in the Andean villages to impose a mode of relating to the world based on scientific and technical knowledge. It is not there to propitiate a dialogue of knowledges nor to promote native knowledge. The community knows this very well and recognizes the role of the school as a bridge to better connect with the modern official world. For this reason, the peasant community has never asked for reforms toward a cognitive plurality in the school environment. The community wants the school to teach modern science and technology independently of the method as long as the educational task is carried out with proficiency. Experience has shown them that this learning is possible. Many children of the community are presently professionals who graduated from higher educational establishments.

Their complaint is the the lack of respect that some young students show toward community traditions, and the lack of interest of some teachers in teaching well, not for the contents itself nor for the method adopted. Stricter teaching modes are even demanded.

Despite the critiques that many intellectuals make of the contents, methods, and philosophy underlying education, the community itself has never asked for curricular reform. This has always been an external action initiated by educational reformers. It is known that the school erodes local knowledge and thus fosters cultural homogeneity. There are profound diagnoses of the school and its role in reproducing an unequal, unjust, and alienating system. Nothing, however, of what has been written has modified the attitude of the communities in their demand for more education. There would thus appear to be a point of coincidence between UNESCO's purposes and those of the Andean communities. Both demand "education for all."

For communities of nurturers like the Andean, there exists no division between what is nurtured and and what is not. From their cosmovision, everything is nurturance and everybody nurtures. In this sense and even though school originates in a nonnurturing culture, for the Andean peoples that does not mean that it cannot be nurtured. Indeed, this is the experience in many places. Nurturing the school is not only buildings and housing for the teachers. To nurture the school is to make it sensitive toward the activities that the community undertakes, it is to make it also part of its life cycle, it is to make it—like the saints—*chacarera*, and to incorporate it, within its possibilities, to the system of authorities in the communal festivities.

These activities must be appreciated as a mode of nurturing diversity. Nurturance does not imply forgetting, cancelling, or annulling one of the cognitive traditions—the scientific and technical. Nor does it propose that Andean knowledge is the only valid approach. Rather, nurturance accepts the pluralistic cultural environment of the community—making the school ampler, more varied, and open toward the heterogeneous and plural. The community can do this by showing the diversity of forms of life in their chacras and encouraging the teacher's affection for it. The community encourages a way of living the joy of the events by offering the school the opportunity of participating in the nurturing traditions of the community. The community, by offering this, is not interested in changing the school but in making it more permeable to nurturance and diversity.

If a nurturer does not divide the world into two realms, nurturance and nonnurturance, but lives her world as a place for nurturance, contradiction does not arise from her own cosmovision. The difference between the mode in which her knowledge is expressed and the mode of the school does not lead her to establish opposition or exclusion but to extend the spectrum of knowledge diversity. Establishing opposite poles, in the manner that characterizes Western-style schools, leads to placing one of the poles as the model with respect to the other, thus representing them as contradictory rather than as complementary. For example, the teaching of modern mathematics demands the annulment of Andean traditions by representing them as superstitions and beliefs that preclude seeing the geometric forms in the world. By this means, there emerges the paradigm, the archetype, the reference that becomes the standard for comparing and contrasting, which leads to judgments about which is superior and which is inferior. These two options lead to the assimilation, colonization, and destruction of what is judged as inferior. History shows how this leads to a forced homogeneity that lends enormous service to a power whose continuous reproduction is only possible to the extent that diversity is obliterated.

Diversity, instead, demands consensus, dialogue, nurturance, equivalence, digestion, symbiosis, inclusion. Andean peasants are accustomed to conversing with a plurality of situations, and their mode of being is that of extending diversity, not of limiting it. As we have shown, each person is a community in herself. From our perspective, this explains the persistence of churches, the school, and the technical advisors of the Green Revolution, among other external agents, in the area of the communities. In a nonfundamentalist culture there is no unique truth. Our cultures are oral and there are no sacred books announcing unquestionable truths. Here, everything is circumstantial and changing.

But change is experienced not as a dialectical struggle on the basis of the existence of opposites, but as the emergence of forms contained in each being. However, the conversations are not always harmonious; some of them can even be violent. Conflict emerging in life is not denied but digested in nurturance, dissolving it ritually and in community in circumstances agreed on by the community. The differences are not translated into opposition and in the emergence of opposites. The communities do not make a problem out of the difference but a possibility of nurturing the diverse.

It is from this communal perspective that we assume the possibility of a different pedagogy, a pedagogy of, and for, diversity so that nature can also have her place. Peasants do it in their own way, a manner that has to be conserved and made more variable also within the classes. The peasants teach us that it is not necessary to cancel or denigrate a form of knowledge in order to show, nurture, and teach another. There is no natural basis for it to happen. In the school, the opposition and annulment of the nurturing of the differences has been introduced to promote forcefully, in replacement, the learning of an exclusive form of conceiving the relationships between humans and nature. Another thing to learn from the peasants is to avoid the colonization of a single plant species in the whole of the chacra. The peasant makes the dominant vegetation thin so that diversity can emerge. This thinning does not imply the elimination of the colonizing plant but its presence within allowable limits and in healthy tuning with the rest of the plants. All peasant experience is saturated with plurality.

An accompaniment to this thinning within the limits of the school implies the mental decolonization of the teachers, because it is obvious that it is not the students who are the agents of cultural erosion, but those who teach within the Western tradition. The peasants show the teachers that the cultivation of native potatoes does not exclude the hybrid varieties. This is a practical way of showing different techniques and knowledge and to sensitize them to respect diversity. But this does not appear to be enough. Teachers, for the most part, do not seem capable of listening and seeing other forms of dialogue with life. It seems that something that is represented as a certainty would require prolonged doses of conscientization; that is, of questioning the modern truths learned in the higher educational establishments as unquestionable. We all need to appreciate the relativity of all technical and scientific knowledge, and to be open to appreciating the plurality of cognitive traditions.

This activity, in our opinion, requires being invigorated and open to the modalities of cooperation exhibited by the nurturers. It is here that we see the important contribution of other people in the thinning and decolonizing tasks that peasants carry out. In this case, the task of decolonization is situated in the domain of knowledge, that is, in the minds of the teachers and all those who have spent many years in the educational system. The challenge resides in clarifying the nature of the mental colonization perpetuated by schools and universities, and beginning the decolonization task by unlearning the metaphysical principles on which rational knowledge is based. It is probable that if we can achieve the decolonization caused by Western forms of education, the cultural assumptions underlying Freire's approach to consciousness raising, we would be better able to perceive what the chacra nurturers do daily.

Contradictions, the knowledge to be masters and owners of nature, experimentation, the cult of the rational, and science and other principles that reside in the very nature of modern teaching are implanted and reproduced, as we know, by the educational system. For us, unlearning means, paradoxically, to relearn them because what we have as scientific knowledge is second-hand knowledge. Unlearning means to return to the lived experience, but in the critical mood that Freire demanded with respect to magical knowledge. This time, however, we have to ask ourselves if the origin of such constructs and their contexts are valid for all, or if there are other ways of naming the life-nurturing processes. Unlearning does not necessarily lead to understanding that the "one" of the metrical system is not inferior or superior to the *juk* (one and its pair) of the Quechua language, but to two different ways of understanding life. For the first, the number was invented, for the second the *quipu* of cords, but both do not need to be placed on the steps of the same cognitive ladder. They are two ways of naming quantities that respond to different cosmovisions. The times now require a dialogue of knowledge and not imposition. Universalism or relativism is a false dilemma.

This is an urgent task in the Peruvian Andes and a needed contribution for cultural affirmation and in the regeneration of diversity. That is, the need is to promote in teachers and all of us an openness to the understanding of a diverse world that needs heterogeneity, where anthropocentrism so rooted in humanism gives way to propositions that lead to the emergence of a pedagogy that strengthens the diversity of culture and nature.

To nurture the school is to nurture the decolonization in each one of us. It is to make us friends of all traditions and not only of scientific knowledge, as the Delors Report demands. But it must be understood, too, that the nurturance of the school is not the making of newly enlightened people, nor of postmodern vanguards. It is a patient activity of the peasants that we support with no other intention than accompanying them in this task of making the chacra shine in all its forms and modalities. As they say, what matters is that the landscape shines, and this task cannot be limited to the agricultural chacra or that of the llamas and alpacas or to the fox's chacras. The school is for the peasant also and, in its own way, a chacra that has to be nurtured so that the landscape of diversity shines.

REFERENCE

Eliot, T. S. (1934). *The rock*. London: Faber and Faber.

3

Who Are the Oppressed?

Bárbara Loyda Sánchez Bejarano

Translated and edited
by Frédérique Apffel-Marglin

I came to Freirian Popular Education in my early years as a militant political activist dedicated to the revolutionary project of transforming the society of Bolivia. Popular education was then seen as necessary in order to create peasant revolutionary cadres. In this sense, Popular Education was a tool to be used to create the conditions necessary for revolutionary change, just like the newspaper as well as propaganda for the work of agitation and organization had been for Lenin. This is why we adopted Popular Education; not just because the majority of its theoreticians understood it as political education.

I began my close association with Popular Education (PE) around 1983. Before that date, I had already had the opportunity to observe some of the methodologies used in PE, such as role playing, and even then it had struck me that the advocates of PE underestimated the capacity of the "popular sectors" to develop a revolutionary consciousness or to fully understand the proposals advanced by the revolutionary vanguard. Nevertheless, until then I had considered that the program of revolutionary change had justice on its side inasmuch as the vanguard's interpretation of the "historical interests" of the peasantry was sufficient for enabling the latter to "follow its lead." Along with other comrades, we carried out political work with peasants over several years. This work was undertaken after the massacres carried out by the dictatorship of Banzer—who was then the democratic president of Bolivia—in 1972. This political work was initiated in Argentina and Peru while I was exiled there. Many of us—leaders of the revolutionary movement and peasants—had fled there after the 1972 massacres and persecutions. Exile forced me to look for other options in the field of pedagogy and teaching among the peasantry, activities that were seen as necessary given their status as "illiterates." My later involvement as a consultant with various development projects provided other experiences that led to further reflections about the methodology and underlying assumptions of PE when applied in other cultural contexts.

Over the course of my years as a popular educator, it became clear to me that Paulo Freire's pedagogy of the oppressed was not able to overcome the hierarchical relationship between the Party and the masses, what Freire himself would call the educator and the oppressed. In my view, such a failure—in spite of what the Freirians claim—is the inevitable result of the underlying worldview of historical materialism (namely the "scientific theory of history"), which considers itself superior to all other views precisely because it is scientific. What enabled me to uncover the imperialist character of this way of seeing other cultures as well as nature was not only my political and development experience but also, later, my discovering the publications of PRATEC (the Andean Project for Peasant Technologies)—the Peruvian NGO (non-governmental organization) that is working to revitalize Andean cultural practices and knowledge essential to sustaining the biodiversity of the region. The publications of PRATEC enabled me to share life experiences with families from Andean campesino communities in my country, Bolivia, in a way that the Freirian pedagogy I had practiced for several years never allowed me to express. Through my new ability to share the campesinos' daily practices and customs, their life and cosmology, these campesino families began to decolonize my mind. They showed me that oppression and the need for change arises from the fact that we ourselves are colonized into thinking of the world "as it ought to be" and not as it is, thus letting our lives be trapped by the notion of the future, a notion that prevents us from living in the present.

FROM LENIN AND THE THEORY OF THE PARTY OF THE CADRES TO FREIRE AND POPULAR EDUCATION

From 1971 to 1980, political organizational work in Bolivia was carried out under a repressive dictatorship that resulted in many persons being exiled, imprisoned, murdered, and/or tortured. The political organizations in general worked clandestinely. In 1964, I accompanied my mother to vote in the last democratic election for a long time to come. I myself voted for the first time in 1978. At that time, the elections were cancelled because another coup d'état had taken place. It was only in 1982 that a democratic regime managed to be installed in Bolivia, a country inhabited by the Quechua and Aymara as well as 30 other distinct cultural groups. The coming of democracy opened a different space for political work that resulted in greater freedom for the exchange of ideas, discussions, and debates. There had emerged in Latin American movements of national liberation the unrealized democratic objectives of achieving a socialist society. Within these movements, the need for the presence of a clear-thinking vanguard was clearly articulated. Lenin's Theory of a Party of Cadres was never questioned. The following quote from Lenin (1975) articulates the gist of this theory:

> We have said that the workers could not have a social-democratic consciousness. This could only be brought from outside. The history of every nation demonstrates that the working class is only capable, by using exclusively its own energies, of articulating a trade-unionist consciousness, that is to say, the conviction that it is necessary to congregate in unions, struggle against the bosses, demand from the government the promulgation of such or such laws necessary for workers, etc. In contrast, the doctrine of socialism has arisen from

historical, philosophical, and economic theories articulated by intellectuals, by educated men belonging to the propertied classes. By their
social position, the very founders of modern scientific socialism, Marx
and Engels, belonged to the intellectual bourgeoisie. Similarly, the
theoretical doctrine of social-democracy has emerged in Russia totally
independently of the spontaneous growth of the workers' movement,
and it has emerged as a natural and inevitable result of the development of thought among socialist revolutionary intellectuals. (p. 28)

At the center of this theory is the hierarchical relationship between the masses and the cadres. This hierarchy was based on the
levels of consciousness attained, that is, on the different groups'
understanding of the historical process through their correct use of
dialectical conceptual tools. Such a hierarchy was seen as legitimate
as it was based on scientific knowledge, something seen as above
bias and thus above suspicion. As in Russia, this was almost always
in the hands of middle-class intellectuals. At the time of our work,
we perceived this hierarchy as being legitimate as well as necessary
in order to guarantee the directionality of the historical materialist
process. We did not see this as an imperialist move in spite of what
had been happening inside as well as outside of the movement and in
the socialist countries, such as the Stalinist purges, the Sino-Soviet
split, Prague 1968, Afghanistan 1974, and Tibet 1955.

Paulo Freire and all the tendencies within PE agreed with Lenin on
the fundamental issues, namely that the laboring or peasant masses
were not able to achieve a consciousness of change on their own.
This is the reason for the need to conscienticize them about their
historical mission, their place in the world, so that they could become
the agents of their own liberation. Freire's program is nearly the same
as Lenin's, with the difference being that Freire made the process
a participative one, which to his followers seemingly overcame the
difficulty of a correct method of thinking that "must be brought from
the outside." Yet his participative method contains an ambiguity
about the emergence of a revolutionary consciousness arising from
the masses themselves. In Freire's (1969) own words:

Once again people, challenged by the dramatic character of the current hour, propose themselves as a problem. They discover that they

know little about themselves, of "their place in the cosmos," and they set themselves to learn more. In addition, *in the recognition of how little they know about themselves* lies one of the reasons for this search. . . . The pedagogy of the oppressed, the one that must be constructed with them and not for them, both persons as well as groups, in the permanent struggle for the recuperation of their humanity. . . . The great problem lies in how the oppressed, as dual beings, inauthentic ones, who "host" the oppressor within themselves, can participate in the articulation of a pedagogy for their liberation. This can be achieved only in so far as they discover that they are "hosting" the oppressor. . . . Such a practice, therefore, implies that the approach to the popular masses be done in such a way as not to bring them a message, but to dialogue with them, get to know them, not only the objectivity in which they encounter each other but rather the consciousness of this objectivity, that is to say, the various levels of perception they have of themselves and of the world in which and with which they are. (p. 87; italics added)

Freire (1969) understood culture as representing "levels of consciousness," and because of this he suggests the recognition of these different levels:

This is the reason that we can not, unless it is done naively, hope to get positive results from an educational program in a more technical sense or of political action, that does not respect the particular world view that the people have or may have. Without this, the program becomes a kind of cultural invasion, perhaps carried out with the best of intentions, but nevertheless a cultural invasion. . . . For this very reason, many times, educators and politicians speak without being understood. Their language is not attuned to the concrete situation of the people they are speaking to. And their speech is one more discourse, alienated and alienating. (pp. 87–88)

Freire's assumption about the stages of cultural development, which he identified as *semi-intransitivity of consciousness, naïve transitivity,* and *critical transitivity,* is the linchpin of a pedagogy that was to move people from the stage where "men . . . cannot apprehend problems situated outside their sphere of biological necessity" to the stage of critical consciousness (pp. 17–18). The appropriate didactical methodologies included readings, participatory techniques, self-diagnoses, participative research, and planning. However, this reformulation did not take into consideration the campesinos' own worldviews because it is assumed that:

> . . . there is no true dialogue if there does not exist in its subjects a true thinking. A critical thought that while not accepting the dichotomy between world and people, recognizes between these two an unshakable solidarity. This is a thought that perceives reality as a process, that captures it as a constant becoming and not as something static. Thought does not dichotomize itself from action and it is permanently immersed in temporality, whose risks it does not fear. (Freire, 1969, p. 84)

Both Lenin and Freire, and along with them the revolutionary parties and movements of all latitudes, agree on the notion that for people or "the masses" to liberate themselves, they must acquire a certain way of thinking, the theory of the vanguard. For Lenin, this vanguard theory was to be formulated by men of the vanguard. For Freire, critical thinking would arise from the dialogue between educators and the peasants who were being encouraged to participate in their own liberation. In both cases, however, the path of what and how to think was determined beforehand. This is how Freire (1969) articulates this point:

> The programmatic content of education is neither a gift nor an imposition—a series of documents that should be deposited in the educating—rather it is the organized, systematized, and *augmented* transfer to the people of those elements that had been provided by the people in an instrumented form. (p. 85; italics added)

From this perspective, all manners of perceiving the world that fall outside of the dialectical method are necessarily inferior. This is alluded to by Freire when, in his *Pedagogy of the Oppressed* (1969), he refers to something Mao said to the French writer Malraux: "Vous savez que je proclame depuis longtemps, nous devons enseigner aux masses avec précision ce que nous avons reçu d'elles avec confusion. [You know that I have proclaimed for a long time that we must teach to the masses with precision what we have received from them confusedly]" (p. 45). In this sense I consider that Freire's Popular Education embodied Lenin's theory of the Cadres Party, which was being adapted by the leaders of other revolutionary movements that arose in Latin America. Latin America is made up of countries with small middle classes, a small proletarian class, but vast "peasant masses" or indigenous peoples. Freire's Popular Education, in spite of his critique of "banking education," is both imperialistic and reactionary and thus unable to resolve the contradictions between the desire to not be invasive culturally by not imposing a particular form of knowing and the desire to empower the oppressed by teaching them to adopt a Western pattern of emancipatory thinking. What Freire and his followers overlooked is that the latter establishes from the start a hierarchical relationship with non-Western cultures. By making critical reflection the only reliable method of knowing, Freire's approach to emancipation has the ironic effect of negating all other forms of being and of living in the world. This is how Freire (1969) puts it:

> We simply cannot reach the workers, whether urban or campesinos (the latter in general immersed in a colonial context, almost umbilically connected to the natural world of which they feel to be a part rather than its transformers) in order to hand them "knowledge" as was done in a banking conception of education, or to impose on them a model with a "good name" in a program whose content we ourselves have organized. (pp. 85–86)

What Freire and his followers did not make explicit is that his pedagogy was based on the assumption that it contained the formula that would enable others to understand "how the world is" and in what way and to what extent it must be transformed. This is the original formulation by Engels (1975):

> . . . for dialectics, which conceives of things and their conceptual images essentially in their connections, in their concatenation, in their dynamics, in their genesis and their demise, processes such as those postulated are no more than other confirmations of its genuine mode of operation. Nature is the touchstone for dialectics, and we must point out that modern natural sciences provide as a proof of this a conjunction of extraordinarily copious data enriched with every passing day, demonstrating with them that in nature, in the last instance, everything occurs in a dialectical mode and not metaphysically, that

it does not move in the eternal monotony of a cycle constantly re-
peating itself, but rather that its trajectory is a true history. . . . Only
following the dialectical path, never losing sight of the general actions
and reactions of genesis and demise, the changes of advance and
retreat, do we arrive at an exact understanding of the universe and of
the development of humanity, as well as of the image projected in the
minds of men. (p. 33)

The road to travel toward a better world was thus clear to us. Armed
with more or less these same notions, we went "to the masses" with
our liberating message. We will see what this implies in the case of
Andean cultures that live the world in a very different way.

THE WORLD REPRESENTED
BY THOUGHT AND THE
LIVING ANDEAN WORLD

The way in which we developed tasks and activities with campesino
communities was through the use of workshops, meetings, and conversations. These improved radically in their dynamics and in the
quality of the contact with the people when we used the methodological contributions of PE. The PE structured these activities according to the dialectical methodological conception that establishes
three phases in the pedagogical process: action–reflection–action.
These were key words in the continuous process that the masses had
to go through in their ascent toward a revolutionary consciousness.
The three-phase process consisted in starting from the practices
of the campesino organizations in order for them to locate these
practices in a larger context through deepened reflection. The last
phase consisted in returning to the practices with a heightened clarity concerning the position of these change agents in the context of
their society. This process, it was assumed, would result in connecting these change agents with "their class" as well as with the whole of
the exploited people in the country.

Normally this was done in workshops where "starting from practical experience" was extracted through participative techniques and
dynamics. These participation techniques, it was believed, would en-

able the campesinos to make explicit, and thus be able to reflect on, the cultural patterns that were part of their taken-for-granted world. By making explicit the experiences of the masses, it would then be possible to elevate their level of revolutionary consciousness. This would require the utilization of the Western approach to reflection and analysis.

What normally occurred in these workshops was that when the campesinos were asked to describe the patterns of their daily experience, they responded in a manner that incorporated the immediacy of their lives with its conflicts and preoccupations pertinent to life in a particular community and time. Issues having to do with irrigation, agriculture, family problems, and everything else that was part of their experience became the focus of their conversation. They were unable to abstract their practices as phenomena that occurred more generally, independently of the particular circumstances of the moment. Many times the workshop turned into a community meeting, where the educator (facilitator or moderator) had nothing to do, her role having been overtaken by the leadership of the community.

The process of identifying the "starting from practices" phase would often be prolonged, sometimes indefinitely. This was a process that we, the educators, understood and designed as only a moment in the consciousness-raising process and not the whole of it. Very seldom did the communities spontaneously follow the process designed for them by us. When they recalled a past event, they did not respond to it as a memory—a past event. Rather, they relived the event with all the intensity with which it had originally happened. They relived the experiencing of feelings and emotions in such a way that we felt embarrassed to enter into their intimacy and invade it as they would not keep anything from us.

The years of promoting literacy and a critical transformative form of consciousness led to other experiences that Freire's theory had not prepared us for. For example, one of our activities was participatory research that generated the issues and arguments for the processes that were to be encouraged. For us, this was supposed to take the form of self-diagnosis. Today, I can see there was no "self" in this self-diagnosis process as it was almost always directed toward what we wanted to know in order to foster a revolutionary consciousness within the campesinos.

Reflecting now on these experiences of "self-diagnosis," I would like to recount an anecdote, which at the time came as a big blow and completely disoriented me. In a community meeting in Bellavista in the Department of Cochabamba (Central Bolivia), we carried out the exercise of self-diagnosis by identifying in great detail the most important problems in the community. When the discussion came around to what was, for the community, the most pressing problem to resolve, it turned out to be the organization of the Festival of the Virgin of the Rosary, the patron saint of the community, which fell in that very month of October. We did not know what to do with our mandate to deepen and seek the causes of the current problem and how to find a solution to it in this case. This Festival was not exactly the problem we had hoped they would identify. The phase of deepening the process of critical reflection was redirected by the community to the preparation of the festival, whereas the phase of the dialectic that was supposed to lead to transforming oppressive practices became the carrying out of the festival itself. We were invited to participate, but as far as our planning for revolutionary change was concerned, it had become totally superfluous.

REFLECTION THAT BECOMES DISCONNECTED FROM THE ACTION IT IS BORN FROM

In order to achieve a deepening of the understanding of a phenomenon in the dialectical paradigm, it is necessary to abstract it from the immediate circumstances in order to be able to grasp it historically as well as logically, situating it in the global context of the class struggle. This mental operation is what enables or allows one to elevate the level of a class consciousness "for itself" to a class consciousness "in itself." This is how Freire (1969) formulates this:

> The great problem lies in how the oppressed, as dual and inauthentic beings who "host" the oppressor within themselves, can participate

in the articulation of the pedagogy for their own liberation. Only to the extent that they discover themselves as "hosting" the oppressor. . . . At the moment in which a critical perception is established in the action itself, a climate of hope and confidence develops that leads people to struggle to overcome "limit situations." Such overcoming which does not exist outside of human–world relations, can only be verified through the actions of people on the concrete reality in which the "limit situations" are found. (p. 47)

In our workshops, this reflection or in-depth thinking phase was carried out with techniques of analysis and abstraction according to Freire's dialectical vision of life. The in-depth thinking phase thus transformed itself into a manner of channeling the reasoning of the participants in a particular direction through the use of "participative" techniques. These techniques were very well structured and elaborated so that the participants' thinking could be directed to whatever the educator wanted to be the focus of discussion. The whole process as well as where it led were in the hands of the educator, which was troubling for me even though we often lacked control over the discussion. Too often, the critical reflection phase became disconnected from daily practices of the campesinos. In addition, when daily practices were identified they, too, often became the basis for the educator to create his own discourse as well as the messages and conclusions that were to be the basis of the campesino's transformed actions. But the campesinos would stay with the immediacy of their lives. They would return over and over again to the present circumstances, looking for answers to the immediate problems they were currently experiencing. Their reflection consisted of giving greater details to the events and the things in their lives, always offering a diversity of criteria, of practices and opinions that were not necessarily considered to be the final word or the correct version. Rather, they were all articulated as just another opinion. What happened at these meetings were general conversations, exchanges of opinions without trying to achieve a consensus or to draw conclusions.

As educators we were outsiders, unable to participate in their community-centered conversations. Furthermore, we were not capable of going along or accompanying such a way of being together. We were not prepared for the diversity and heterogeneity of the ways of being and doing that campesinos experienced on a daily basis. Instead of dialogue, the conversation between them and ourselves ran along parallel lines that most of the time never crossed or met.

They had no desire to go anywhere, whereas we felt that the only way to live required adopting a dialectical form of consciousness. What I understood was that the dialectical formula of action–reflection–action corresponds to a way of thinking about the world where it is possible to project the future through a series of mental operations. In the case of PE, based as it was on the notion of a dialectical methodology, our mission was to lead the campesinos to embrace a socialist future—which is far from their daily reality. In other words, we were trying to lead them to transform themselves in order to achieve the ideal world that was better than the one they were living in right now. And what gave our mission its moral authority were the universal laws supposedly expressed in a dialectical way of thinking.

Today I am able to understand the contrast between my experiences of doing workshops in campesino communities and doing them with campesinos in the city. In the city it was easier to conduct workshops because the campesinos were separated from their communities and came from different regions of Bolivia. Thus, their experiences and problems were not held in common, which made is easier for us to channel their thinking toward a global analysis, establishing similarities and differences in order to extract criteria that would form the basis for generalizations.

CADRES AND "CARGOS": LEVELS OF CONSCIOUSNESS

In order to carry forward the historical project of emancipation, it was necessary to "return to the practice" of the actors themselves—in this case the campesino communities. This was the moment when the results of the process were tested and when we could assess whether the required clarity had been achieved. It was also the moment when we could judge the extent to which a revolutionary consciousness had been adopted, and whether others would carry our mission forward. For almost 3 years, we executed a plan to form campesino cadres that were supposed to strengthen a particular union organization in Bolivia called "The Only Union Federation of Campesino Workers of Bolivia" (CSUTCB). The objective was part of a strategy to gain political spaces for a revolutionary option as well as more members for the political organization itself. The plan consisted in organizing courses in which the following subjects were taught: Bolivian History, History of the Campesino and Workers' Union Movement; Analysis of the Laws and the Proposed Laws of the Government; First Aid; and Oratory.

Our goal was to organize these courses for different levels in order to train the political and union cadres. But we never were able to achieve this. Seldom did the same group of campesino comrades attend a particular course. Different campesinos attended the sessions of the same course. In subsequent conversations, we found out that the community was not accustomed to the notion of always having the same person attend the course because "everyone should have the opportunity to learn." Whereas our approach was based on the assumption of individual decision making and responsibility, the real authority in these campesino communities is exercised through the *cargos*. The cargo is a service that every community member (which often involves the entire family) renders to the community as a whole on a rotating basis. It was on that basis that they attended the training courses.

The problem for us was how to develop the different levels of consciousness in order to produce qualified and politically conscious cadres that would strengthen the political effectiveness of the union. In order to develop the cadre, it was necessary to transform the campesino into the Western type of individual who is capable of thinking abstractly about the world and the changes it must undergo. This required individuals who could compare themselves with the well-being of others of their oppressed class and with the classes above them. This way of understanding, we thought, would lead them to struggle to improve their situation. A brotherly bond with other individuals would ensure progress for all.

What we came to understand is that in the Andean tradition, the cargos do not create hierarchies within the community. Hierarchies are not needed because the campesinos do not conceive of their lives apart from the community, that is, apart from their relationship with others. Everything is done communally. The cargo in campesino communities involves lending service to the community. For those who exercise a cargo, and for their families, it means to take on a special responsibility for the whole community. Every family knows that at some point in time, it will be their turn to exercise a cargo and they make their best effort to fulfill their special responsibility. There are as many cargos as there are spheres of life, and these spheres are not hierarchically ordered. They are all important and necessary for the regeneration of life. Thus, for example, the Water Judge is as important as the Jarrero, and their respective responsibilities depend on the time and the circumstance. The Jarrero is the person in charge of looking after the chacras (the peasants' cultivated small fields) and determines the time when they need to be irrigated. He observes and determines which chacras as well as which crops need irrigation the most. He then informs the Water Judge about which chacras must be irrigated first and at what time. Who is the boss here, the Water Judge or the chacra? Who is the authority? Who has made the decision?

With a colleague and friend, Marina Arratia, we conducted research on the cultural practices surrounding the process of irrigation in an Andean community in Bolivia and came to the following thoughts concerning the nature of the cargos:

> Centralized and all embracing power has no place in a world where all are equal beings, thus authority does not mean expropriation or having control of power. The obligatory rotation of the cargos for each community member and the annual renewal of these cargos is a wise prevention against the accumulation of power. Therefore there does not exist either laws or permanent institutions that are indispensable and that cannot be removed. In a changing and dynamic world there is no room for permanent decisions. What we have instead is a permanent conversation with the ever-changing circumstances that recreates everything. . . . The way of exercising authority is through the cargo, a service that seeks to harmonize the interests of everyone which for this reason is charismatic in nature. Its role is to enliven the conversation and the dialogue in order to reach agreements. The agreements are the basis for immediate action and these are renewed

permanently according to the contingency of the moment. This allows for doing the most pertinent things at each moment and according to each circumstance. There are no decisions taken, in the strict sense of the word, but rather momentary agreements that are the fruits of permanent conversations. (Sánchez & Arratia, 1997, p. 8)

Sometimes the courses we offered were done in response to a request by a community. We found we could never work with the "leaders" or the "enlightened" members of the community because invariably almost everyone in the community showed up for the course. Several difficulties would arise in these cases. Imagine working with 100 or 150 people or more! That was unmanageable. Everyone would come including men, women, children, and elders. They would come with their food or would cook there and stay the entire day. These were events taking place in *their* community to which they did not need an invitation. It concerned them all and so they all came.

In this context, political differences did not seem important. Everyone's opinion was heard without anyone getting upset. The campesinos would say what was on their minds without anyone becoming angry. Critical reflection or in-depth analysis, however, was not achieved, nor were any conclusions reached about transforming practices. Everything was valid. The community emerged for us. We discovered it in the course of the communal workshops, and little by little it communicated to us its wisdom. We gradually discovered a world beyond formality, a way of being in the world. Our own world was filled with injustices, whereas the world of the campesino communities was not. The campesino community lives in constant reciprocity, with a constant exchange of responsibilities and services. It lives as a permanent fiesta from planting to harvesting. The absence of categories and hierarchies in the campesino community initially made it difficult for us to grasp, given our Western way of thinking. The Freirean Western conceptual tools that we had acquired were useful for uncovering relations of power, stratification patterns, and other socioeconomic differentiations. But we had to unlearn this Western way of thinking in order to learn about everything from the campesino approach to house building, the long labors of agriculture and of animal husbandry, irrigation, road maintenance, baptisms, to marriages and funerals. In all of these tasks, mutual help was central. In such a context, a festival or a funeral has the same weight as a state law. The particular issue at hand is less important than the fact that every member of the community is committed to participating in every task, every event.

What can be done when the participants cannot abstract them-selves from their lives so as to think it, when they simply just live it? What can de done with people for whom what we want to separate as a moment or a point of departure contains all at once the present, past, and future? How are we to raise the consciousness of a people who only live according to each set of circumstances—people who base their lives on conversations and on the harmony between the members of their community, which include not only the humans but also the nonhuman world of nature and its deities? This was impossible; we began to sense that something did not work and that it was not a case of misapplying Freire's methodology. Rather, it was our whole way of thinking, with its goals, purposes, and methods that proved so inadequate when confronted with these people so different from us. As we learned from the community, we began to unlearn the thought world, constructed on the basis of mental abstractions.

SOME REFLECTIONS

The initial feelings that made us reject the instituted order because it was unjust also brought us close to "the people," but our ideology drove us apart. The first were feelings, whereas the latter were more premeditated. The vanguards, the individual women and men who constitute them, need to rationalize their rebellion in order to re-main in the vanguard for many years, because it would be impossible for them to do so otherwise. The dialectical method teaches us that revolution is not only necessary but also possible. This explains why the female members of the vanguard remain alone. They are always found on the barricades because they do not have anything else to do. The people are interested in living. Sometimes they make a pause in order to improve life but they do not spend their time improving life but rather living it. The vanguards, on the other hand, live for the struggle itself and life outside of it is meaningless. They are trapped by their mission and oppressed by the ideology of "what ought to be." The only thing that can explain such a way of life "bereft of the present," and tormented by the mission of saving others, is blind confidence.

Our political action as cadres included a personal commitment that was based on the faith that the world functions on the basis of universal laws that are leading humanity on a path of continual progress. This meant that the social transformation was seen as not only necessary but also possible to achieve through the working out of these laws. The issue of personal commitment—although it is not the central theme of this chapter, it is tangential to it—deserves a few words. Today I see it as a questionable altruism. I see it as being somehow the leitmotif of the revolutionaries that is rationalized as a scientific theory, while at bottom it is nothing but the despair that arises when one does not find one's place in the established order. Only this can explain why we do not notice important details.

What I have understood over these years is that those whom we thought of as the main victims of colonial oppression, namely the workers and the campesinos, were in fact not the victims, rather that we were the oppressed ones. We were the dissatisfied ones, anxious to project our consciousness onto the masses in order to change our position in a world that did not fit us. Starting from the practices of the masses, perhaps this starting point that PE recovered from the classics (and that had been lost in the work of the vanguards) and that it recuperated through a creative, cheerful pedagogy very appropriate in our context, has been the best of PE. This has been the opening for me, along with my reading of the works of PRATEC, to being able to communicate with the Andean campesino world and discover it while living it.

Freire's methods have succeeded to the point where they are now the basis for a globalizing education and system of governance. He and his followers have recreated pedagogy. But whom does this pedagogy serve? This is a theme for another debate. In reality, his PE simply remained an instrumental revision of pedagogy because in practice it was never able to transcend the hierarchy implicit in intellectual activity. The intellectual activity of critical reflection was seen as the correct path for living and perceiving the world, even when confronted with other modes of living and perceiving such as those of the Andean campesinos. The hierarchy implicit in Freire's pedagogy has its roots in other hierarchical relationships in the West: between the party and the masses, soldiers and officers, workers and campesinos, party leadership and the base. The seizure of power, when it is based on hierarchical patterns of authority, transforms relationships into what some call the bureaucratic bourgeoisie culture.

But it has also damaged the notion of participation, a myth that has simply let itself become institutionalized and that has legitimized marginality. In order for this myth to justify itself, it has no other choice—as with the vanguards—but to base the necessity of its existence on the needs of the poor. The distance between educator and oppressed never ceases to exist as a relationship of power. Ever since Marx's famous/infamous writings concerning the necessity, even if a painful one, for the British to conquer and destroy India in order to wrest it out of its superstitious historical slumber and put it on the path of progress, revolutionary thinkers in the West have assumed that it is also necessary to nonrationally based cultures for them to achieve the utopian vision that has eluded the revolutionary reformers in the West.

In contrast, Andean campesinos lovingly nurture everything that exists in the Pacha [the local place/time], the chacras, the trees, the mountains, the pastures, the springs, because all are sacred and worthy of nurturance. Their deities are not idols, but rather living beings that protect us and nurture us, and with whom one converses and who are also cared for. In this world of equivalencies and incompleteness, we all fit and we do not need a reason for being simply because we exist and that is enough. We have all been nurtured by the campesinos in many days of workshops, fiestas and rituals, in that patient and caring way that only they know how to do.

Being unable to resolve the contradictions in Freire's approach to popular education, I now work to promote intercultural learning as a campesino nurturing project. Accompanying them and learning from them in their nurturing processes is our greatest ambition, and it is today our modest path.

REFERENCES

Engels, F. (1975). *Anti Dühring.* Edit. pueblo y educación, La Habana.

Freire, P. (1969). *Pedagogía del oprimido, 1969.* Edit. estudiantil, Cochabamba.

Freire, P. (1973). *Educacion para una conciencia critica.* Ediciones la aurora.

Lenin, V. I. (1975). *¿Qué hacer?* Edit. Progreso, Moscú.

Sanchez, L., & Arratia, M. (1997). *Género y Riego en Comunidades Campesinas de los Andes: Una aproximación conceptual.* PRONAR occasional papers, Cochabamba, Bolivia.

4

Vernacular Education for Cultural Regeneration: An Alternative to Paulo Freire's Vision of Emancipation

Gustavo A. Terán

> Our genius lies in our capacity to make meaning through the creation of narratives. . . . The measure of a narrative's "truth" or "falsity" is in its consequences: does it provide people with a sense of personal identity, a sense of community life, a basis for moral conduct, explanations of that which cannot be known?
> —Postman (1995, p. 9)

Social scientist Benjamin Barber tells us that "education is systematic story-telling" (1987, p. 22). Education provides us with a narrative that defines our role in society. Formal education in America attempts to instill in us a common set of values, a way of understanding the world and acting in it. But which story is ours? Who are the "We" that lay claim to the story that defines us as Americans? Who decides which story or stories will be taught in school, whose knowledge or preferences count, and what criteria will be used to assess these preferences?

In a multicultural society, educational practice must be informed by the many different narratives that define our diverse cultural heritage. And yet, in most pluralist societies where many cultures coexist, educational institutions tend to promote one story. From my perspective, the core values that lie beneath the surface of cultural patterns, that inform different cultures' understanding of the world, have been largely ignored in our educational agenda. Notwithstanding multicultural and bilingual education initiatives, my experience has been that many of the ceremonies, rituals, and family practices that tied generations together in the Mexican-American communities of South Texas, where I grew up, have been largely abandoned. Chad Richardson (1999), director of the Border-life Project at the University of Texas in Edinburg, documents similar experiences among South Texas border residents. Tina Morales, one of his interviewees, expressed her sense of loss in the following way:

> My parents couldn't stand the way Mexican Americans here had changed their language and their culture to be more like the Anglos. It didn't bother me because I felt we were all just trying to fit in. So I assimilated into the Anglo culture and raised my children in Anglo ways. Lately, I've come to realize that I've lost something. (p. 153)

The "Anglo culture" that Tina bemoans is the patterns of behaviors characterized by individualist and consumerist habits. Tina's and my own experiences support Fischer's (1986) assessment that "late twentieth-century society globally seems to be characterized by surface homogenization, by the erosion of public enactments of tradition, by the loss of ritual and historical rootedness" (p. 197).

Living in the midst of the present consumer-dependent society, embedded in a culture that sees continual change—measured by economic growth and technological innovation—as a reflection of social progress and perceives the individual as the social unit of authority (Bowers, 1995), it is difficult to see what alternatives remain for those who feel thoroughly disaffected with the direction of our current social predicament. This dominant mode of thinking seems to alienate humans from each other and from their environment. Moreover, the objectivist framework that guides education in the West encourages this separation and in so doing contributes to the degradation of the environment and perpetuates an ecological crisis. The emancipating ideologies, including the ideas of Paulo Freire, that once framed my own sense of justice during the Chicano movement of the 1960s and 1970s now seem inadequate for addressing the social and environmental crisis that unfolds before our eyes. Educational theories that promote a single universal solution to the pressing social issues of our time foreclose the possibility of finding alternative paths to the good life. Universal solutions such as emancipation through critical reflection carry the epistemological baggage of their proponents, and thus cannot avoid becoming colonizing events. This is especially the case when the proponents of emancipation, such as Paulo Freire, are Western thinkers and their solutions are being introduced, often with the best of intentions, into non-Western cultures.

Rather than turn to the abstract liberating theories that have informed my thinking and actions for the last 30 years, I look for answers in stories of diverse communities, where local and culturally specific narratives still guide the thoughts and actions of community members. Education as story-telling can help revitalize the diverse narratives that inform pluralist societies and provide guidance in the regeneration of cultural patterns that are more attuned to the social and environmental demands of our times. In this search I am guided by the work of Mexican intellectual and social activist Gustavo Esteva. Esteva opens doors to possible futures through sharing the "living stories" of diverse communities in his home state of Oaxaca. Story-telling in this case means drawing the listener into the story through genuine dialogue and movement with the living characters of the story.

VERNACULAR CULTURE AND EDUCATION

The dominant narratives that have guided education policy in the industrialized countries for the last half-century are the myths of economic development and individual emancipation. Although these myths appear to be in conflict with each other, they both undermine alternative knowledge systems rooted in the traditions of local communities (Howard, 1994). Moreover, as Dirlik (1998) points out, the development myth assumes the cultural superiority of the Western world: "It is a notion of culture [that] has often been used to render place-bound cultural identities into markers of backwardness, which then has provided the excuse for opening them up to 'civilization'—global and national" (p. 6).

This Western narrative of economic development, individualism, and cultural superiority has served as the dominant policy framework in industrialized countries and among elites in less industrially developed countries for the past 50 years. In countries where ethnic and cultural groups still maintain their long-held customs and traditions, however, many groups are beginning to question national governments' imposition of so-called modern values, imported from the industrialized countries (Garcia Canclini, 1995). Working against a sense of fragmentation of core cultural narratives, many communities are seeking to reconstruct their stories, to regenerate those cultural spaces that define and give meaning to their lives (Esteva, 1987, 1993; Fischer, 1986). Told in the vernacular language of local culture, these stories portray the struggles of people to define their lives, to dream their own dreams.

The following story illustrates the power that constructing one's own narrative can have in shaping lives at the grassroots. It is the story of a community in the southern Mexican state of Oaxaca that is resisting the modernizing forces of globalization by creating new political spaces and regenerating their cultural alternatives to modernization (Esteva, 1987). The account that follows is based on my own research in the community of San Martin.

A SPACE ON THE SIDE
OF THE ROAD

Traveling from the city of Oaxaca in the central valleys of the Sierra Occidental mountain range toward the Pacific coast, within an hour

one passes through the village of San Martin. The village is a nonde-
script scattering of houses at the foot of the mountains, surrounded
by large tracts of pasture and fields. The most interesting sight for
passing travelers is probably a curious set of pyramid-shaped buildings
on the side of the road in the outskirts of the village. Once the site of
a federal agricultural project, the abandoned structures are now the
home of what a local group of young men are calling a Vernacular
Education Center (hereafter referred to as the Center). Much like
anthropologist Katherine Stewart's (1996) "space on the side of the
road," which locates vernacular culture in Appalachia to one side of
the main road of dominant "American culture," this Center is set off,
literally and metaphorically, to the side of the Mexican road to development, progress, and modernity. Here one encounters the "other
Mexico" that Mexican anthropologist Bonfil Batalla (1996) calls
"Mexico Profundo," or deep Mexico. As with Steward's Appalachia,
the Center is the door to encounters with otherness in the midst of
the imagined national identity.

On the surface, San Martin does not appear any different from
other rural villages that take their cues for progress from the nearby
metropolis of Oaxaca and beyond that, Mexico City. The signs of
"progress" include a new housing development for federal employees
constructed right in the center of the village and a gated high school/
vocational center that includes a swimming pool. These development projects, however, betray local peoples' struggle to defend their
autonomy and traditional life styles. To the stranger, the only visible
sign of the incredible vitality and spirit of regeneration in the village
may well be the odd set of structures on the outskirts of town. There,
a few yards away from the modern school, stands a place where local
peoples' dreams of a self-sustaining community begin to flourish. This
place is the home of a few native sons, intent on regenerating autonomous spaces for learning and working in and with the community.

REGENERATING PLACE

The Vernacular Education Center is the creation of a group of young
university students who refused to leave their community to pursue

careers in their chosen professions—careers for which they could never find jobs in their own community. These native sons of San Martin, rooted in their community, clearly reflect the hopes of many other young men and women throughout Mexico who are also creating spaces that allow for the regeneration of those traditions and local stories that give meaning to their lives (Prakash & Esteva, 1998). Regeneration here means more than reconstructing local spaces with culturally appropriate means and materials. It means reconnecting with the elders of the community, paying respect to those generations that connect them with their own history, and recognizing the wisdom and knowledge of elders that schools taught them to devalue.

In a recent workshop Doña María, the local traditional healer, was asked to come to the Center to talk to a group of young men and women about medicinal herbs and how to prepare and use them. Doña María proudly displayed her variety of local herbs, carefully explained the curative properties of each, and discussed where and when locally these herbs could be used. She also demonstrated the use of several of the herbs. Afterwards Doña María proudly arranged a tour of her own "clinic" in her house. Along the way, she recounted stories of medical doctors who came to receive treatment in her humble home and of remarkable recoveries from health problems that conventional medicine could not treat.

On another occasion, Don Manuel, a peasant farmer from a neighboring village, came to show the youth how to build a *temezcal*, a kind of sweat lodge used for curative practices. Working with the young men and women in hands-on fashion, Don Manuel demonstrated how the temezcal is built and why it is built that way. As he worked, he explained the curative properties of the temezcal and told stories of other treatments he and his family have found useful—ointments made from snakes and other animals and from rare plants. Many other elders come to the Center to share their knowledge with members of their own and neighboring communities. They describe and demonstrate farming methods, building techniques with adobe and other local materials, animal husbandry, and other skills and knowledge gained through working and living in their villages. And always with this practical knowledge come the stories that place these practices in their cultural and historical context. The young men at the Center clearly demonstrate what their friend and mentor Gustavo Esteva calls the regeneration of the art of living and dying (private conversation).

Regeneration, as noted earlier, means reconnecting with the community. The young members of the Vernacular Education Center explain that as various aspects of modernity invade their lives—such as television, video games, and cell phones—young people have been loosening their ties to the community. Having been brought up in a more traditional lifestyle that values the role of elders and that considers obligation to the community as central to belonging to a specific place, the young men of the Center have fashioned an educational agenda that strives to reconnect youth with community. They do this by contributing to the community—building dry latrines, adobe stoves, fish ponds, and promoting reforestation projects. They do it also by learning from elders and by sharing their own knowledge with the elders. This is how the community begins to recognize them and re-member them as part of the community and they in turn re-member the community by learning and retelling the stories of their elders. *Re-member* here means making members again through a process that remembers history. And local history and the stories are the basis for the construction of an educational agenda that incorporates the dreams and desires of the people at the local level. They are the basis for a vernacular educational agenda.

WHO ARE THESE PROPONENTS OF VERNACULAR EDUCATION?

A group of university friends who felt the need to do something for their community, the organizers of the Center began as an environmental group in 1991. Their first project was the reforestation of the village watershed. Through the years, the group of young men took on other community projects like building lorena (adobe) stoves, repopulation of native quails to the region, and small scale animal production. They restored an abandoned agricultural station and eventually established the present Center. When asked to describe what vernacular education means to them, this is what Marcos, a founding member, has to say:

> We asked ourselves, what is it that we have to do to be truly autono-
> mous; to not only survive economically but to fashion a life that we
> want. Yes, we want to be able to produce our own food and shel-
> ter. But we want to go beyond that, we want to produce our own
> knowledge. We want to organize an educational project—a living
> and learning program—based on local culture. We want a life project
> that makes use of local knowledge enriched by innovative ideas from
> other communities and friends from other places. This experience of
> learning that combines the traditional knowledge of our elders and
> the innovative ideas and technologies of the modern world is what we
> are calling vernacular education. (Terán, 1998, recorded interview)

All of the founding members of the Center have received their university degrees. The group includes two biologists, two veterinarians, an accountant, and an architect. For rural youth, in particular, getting through a university degree program is quite an accomplishment. But like so many other young men and women in Mexico, this group of young people do not pride themselves on a piece of paper that does not guarantee a minimum wage job. Julio, another member of the group, describes their predicament:

> For us, our whole education has really not been very useful or rel-
> evant. We were never taught the things we need to know to be able
> to stay and make a life for ourselves in our village. Education prepares
> us for jobs that don't exist here. It prepares us to abandon our home.
> But we don't want to leave, so we have had to learn by ourselves, with
> friends and with the elders of the community, those things that are
> useful and important for living here. We are learning construction
> techniques, with adobe for example, that were once prevalent here
> but have now largely disappeared. Of course, we are adding innovative
> designs and techniques but that is part of combining the traditional
> with new knowledge. That is what we are calling vernacular educa-
> tion—education for living in our own place. Education for life—for
> fashioning our life projects. (Terán, 1998)

In Mexico more and more young people graduate from schools and universities only to find that there are no jobs or opportunities to practice professions that they thought would give them a decent living. Young people who expected to gather the fruits of their hard-earned degrees discover that much of what they learned has no relevance to life in their village and that they must leave in order to find a job (Esteva, personal conversation). Those young people who decide to stay have nothing to do. Many of them have lost interest in working the land, as it is hard work that leaves little surplus. Others, however, like this group of young men in San Martin, are looking at this crisis as an opportunity, an opportunity to create what they refer to as their "life projects." Marcos explains:

> Our life projects are more than work for survival and sustenance, they are a way of life, a way of thinking. Life projects are the production of our own conscience. Not life defined from outside but on our own terms. We do not only produce food and material goods. We produce ideas. We produce knowledge. We produce our own education. Our philosophy of education is learning through common sense. Learning the things that make sense in our context and learning through doing with our elders but also with friends from outside who share our interests. (Terán, 1998)

In the vernacular education program, graduates do not get a diploma or certificate, rather they discover a life project. It is a life project shaped by knowledge and experience shared by family and friends in a specific community, within a particular culture and with an orientation guided by history and tradition as well as the contingencies of the present moment. The young person does not necessarily preselect a concentration of skills or knowledge to pursue. As education is more than this—it is a life project—they discover their vocation through experiments in communal working and living. The members of the Center see their role as that of providing a rich mix of opportunities for learning and creating a nurturing environment where young people can experiment with the various vocational options. Moreover, traditional knowledge is once more given the value that schools took away. Here, elders become important mentors to the young.

Although not everyone in the village supports a community-based education project that promotes self-sufficiency and traditional knowledge, the young men and the families that support them are well respected in the community. Problems arise, however, when Center members seek support for some of their projects from outside sources. From their perspective, the problem resides in the lack of respect from government representatives and technical experts for place-based, traditional knowledge systems.

LOCAL KNOWLEDGE VERSUS EXPERT KNOWLEDGE

While aspiring to autonomy, the young members of CEV also seek out support for their projects with representatives of state and federal agencies responsible for social and economic development. They also seek out support of artists and intellectuals in the city of Oaxaca and beyond. They find it difficult, however, to make outsiders understand what they are doing and why. Marcos explains it this way:

> Outsiders define us and our situation with language that is foreign to us. They use categories that do not correspond to our reality. We have our own language, our own way of expressing our desires, our interests, and our hopes. We do not recognize ourselves in the description that others have of us. But professionals and intellectuals expect us to accept their description of us, of our "problems"—situations that we do not define as problems. We are perfectly able to define our lives in our own words. We do not need pretty words of intellectuals to know what we are. (Terán, 1998)

As university graduates, Center members obviously understand and can relate to the language of intellectuals and technical experts. They choose, however, to speak with the voice of the older generation, to articulate the sentiments that elders intimate in their daily work with them. The young men themselves, rooted in that local culture, reclaim the vernacular language as their own. The problem of communication with outside experts and intellectuals, however, is more than an issue of language. It is an issue of attitude. Marcos elaborates:

> Intellectuals and experts from outside treat us as if we are simply workers, laborers with no consciousness of our situation, with no intellectual capacity to understand our situation and what is best

for us. They come to advise us, to tell us what we must do. They separated work of the mind from work with the hands. They consider us workers not thinkers. But we do not make that separation. In our work and in our lives we integrate thinking and doing. We are not in need of proper vocabularies and categories to understand our lives and what we must do. What we are in need of is a process whereby we can meet and talk with outsiders and discover together what each has to contribute to any particular project or idea. We need a process for intercultural dialogue. This requires first that outsiders recognized our knowledge, experience and cultural context. (Terán, 1998)

For the Center youth, the relationship with outsiders is not one of equality. They want to remain different, to remain true to their specific cultural context, but they also want to speak to the other from their own place. They want to establish a process of communication that respects differences rather than one that attempts to "win" an argument and impose a "solution" to local "problems." As Marcos puts it:

We want to be able to develop a language for communicating with the outside world that is created through dialogue. When we meet as equals in our discussion we can define what we want, we can describe the world together in a manner that makes sense to us and them, or at least we can agree on some things and accept that we will not agree on other things, and leave those things aside. We will no longer accept a relationship with outside agents, be they government agency representatives or intellectuals, which places us in a subordinate relationship. We will be open to discussion of things we might do together but not to what can be imposed on us. (Terán, 1998)

DIALOGUE AND CO-MOTION

What the young men and their community are articulating is a desire to preserve those aspects of tradition that they consider important and at the same time to open up to other dimensions of truth and beauty that fit within their local context. What the young men of CEV suggest is that the clash that exists in encounters between the purveyors of modernity (technical experts of one kind or another, politicians, and intellectuals) and the bearers of tradition and vernacular knowledge, the peasants, healers, and story-tellers of San Martin, can only be resolved through a communicative process that takes into account the cultural assumptions of each group and that creates a space for mutual respect and reciprocal interaction (Falzon, 1998; Panikkar, 1995; Vachon, 1995).

This process of intercultural dialogue is one that has been introduced to the Center members by Gustavo Esteva. Esteva has been documenting and articulating similar stories of liberation through regeneration of local spaces for many years. Indeed, as a social activist, Esteva not only articulates the processes he observes, he also helps shape the direction of these processes by telling the stories of other communities engaged in similar struggles. This "nomadic storyteller" carries stories that invigorate the local discourse and engages community members in dialogue and action. Going beyond intercultural dialogue, Esteva encourages a type of grassroots movement that respects differences and at the same time provides mutual support. This "co-motion" or moving together, is a notion that Center members have appropriated. Marcos explains:

> Outsiders may look at our projects and say, you don't seem to have accomplished much. I don't see much economic improvement in your lives. There doesn't seem to be that much progress as a result of all your work. What they don't know is that we have gained hope. Most of all what we have gained is that we built a social movement of youth; a movement for autonomy and autonomous learning. We are connecting to other groups. We are moving together in many different directions, supporting each other in our different paths and coming together in a common rejection of those constraints that try to contain our movement. (Terán, 1998)

Here, decision making across communities requires that everyone affected by the decision participates as an equal partner. Decisions are not made among power brokers but by peoples in all the communities affected. This requires a process that goes beyond the usual technological–rational deliberation of managers and experts. It is a process where traditional and vernacular knowledge carries as much weight as scientific or technical knowledge. No one knowledge system is privileged.

Fundamental to this process is a dialogic approach that respects cultural differences. Intercultural dialogue goes beyond conventional dialogue in that it recognizes that people from different cultural traditions bring different sets of assumptions and presuppositions about the world and therefore people come with a sometimes drastically different understanding of the same problem. Whereas one sees a particular problem as a simple case of efficient resource use, others may see it as a case of respect for ancient spiritual grounds or trees or rocks. Intercultural dialogue means that in order to reach some type of agreement, everyone must understand how the other sees the problem. All presuppositions that are generally taken for granted and not seen by their owners must be made explicit—put on the table—so that the deliberative process is informed by the entire universe of concerns at the table. Through authentic intercultural dialogue, it is possible to maintain one's cultural autonomy and at the same time move together toward resolution of those issues that cut across community, region, or state boundaries.

The creation of spaces like the Vernacular Education Center appears as a workable mechanism for mediated movements that regenerate communal spaces. These movements of intracommunal and regional networks represent new ways that people at the grass roots relate to each other. These networks allow communities to maintain their own ways while searching and finding ground for agreement on those matters that transcend community interests and concerns, such as environmental degradation or exploitation and use of the greater environmental commons.

Finally, the Vernacular Education Center represents the type of spaces that communities are creating to come together, young and old, to tell stories and live stories that are meaningful to them and that guide their movement together, stories that allow people to dream their own dreams.

REFERENCES

Barber, B. (1992). An aristocracy for everyone: The politics of education and the future of America. New York: Balantine Books.

Bonfil Batalla, G. B. (1996). *Mexico Profundo: Reclaiming a civilization.* Austin, TX: University of Texas Press.

Bowers, C. A. (1995). *Educating for an ecologically sustainable culture: Re-thinking moral education, creativity, intelligence, and other modern orthodoxies.* Albany, NY: State University of New York Press.

Dirlik, A. (1998). Globalism and the politics of place. *Development, 41* (2). Available: www.sidint.org/publications/development/vol41/no2/41–2b.html

Esteva, G. (1987). Regenerating people's spaces. *Alternatives, 12* (1), 125–152.

Esteva, G. (1993). A new source of hope: The margins." *Interculture 26* (2), 2–62.

Falzon, C. (1998). *Foucault and social dialogue: Beyond fragmentation.* New York: Routledge.

Fischer, M. J. (1986). Ethnicity and the post-modern arts of memory. In J. Clifford & G. Marcus (Eds.), *Writing culture. The poetics and politics of ethnography* (pp. 194–233). Berkeley: University of California Press.

Garcia Canclini, N. (1995). *Hybrid cultures: Strategies for entering and leaving modernity.* Minneapolis, MN: University of Minnesota Press.

Howard, P. (1994). The confrontation of modern and traditional knowledge systems In development. *Canadian Journal of Communication* [On-line serial], *19* (2). Avaliable: http://wlu.ca/~wwwpress/jrls/cjc/BackIssues/19.2/howard.html.

Panikkar, R. (1995). *Invisible harmony: Essays on contemplation and responsibility.* Minneapolis: Fortress Press.

Postman, N. (1995). *The end of education.* New York: Knopf.

Prakash, S., & Esteva, G. (1998). *Grassroots post-modernism. Remaking the soil of cultures.* London: Zed Books.

Richardson, C. (1999). From Mexicans to Mexican Americans. In *Batos, bolillos, pochos and pelados* (pp. 153–182). Austin: University of Texas Press.

Stewart, K. (1996). *A space on the side of the road.* Princeton: Princeton University Press.

Vachon, R. (1995). Guswenta or the intercultural imperative. *Interculture, 28* (2), 1–73.

5

From Conscientization to Interbeing: A Personal Journey

Siddhartha

I remember talking to an untouchable caste laborer outside a village teashop near the city of Madras. I think the year was 1970. He was all deference, seeing me as someone of higher social status than him. He placed the cup of tea he was drinking on the ground and folded his hands in respect, slouching a little in servility. He could drink tea only from an aluminium mug, and only outside the teashop. The glass tumblers were reserved for upper caste clients who sat inside. The untouchable could not enter the shop as his status was too low and he would pollute the others if he did. I tried to provoke him into thinking of the injustice of it all, but our worldviews were very different. What was injustice to me was perfectly normal to him. He was immersed in what Paulo Freire called "the culture of silence." When you cannot "name" your reality, you are unable to grasp why you are poor and who keeps you poor. You accept to be taken for the dregs of society, totally oblivious of what is happening to you and your people. You are paralyzed in a mist of naïve ignorance, the culture of silence.

The assumption that poor and oppressed social classes were enveloped in a world that they could not comprehend was partly true from my experience, but even in those early days I was uncomfortable with the expression "the culture of silence." The peasant or slum-dweller was also a rich repository of wisdom and critical acumen, even if his worldview was a traditional one and very different from the modern liberal or Marxist one. Freire was right to suggest that the oppressed person had to be empowered through reflecting and acting on the structures of oppression. He was wrong in underemphasizing the rich veins of practical and spiritual knowledge that ordinary people possessed. The rest of this chapter continues with my ambivalent attitude toward Freire. While appreciating the role of his ideas in making people aware of class and caste issues and providing an inspiring vision to transform unjust situations, I also dwell on the absence of holism in his thinking. Besides overlooking key social and ecological factors, he also reduces "liberation" to a linear anthropocentric process that overlooks the biosphere.

My involvement with Freire and his ideas began 25 years ago when a small group of university students called the Free University, of which I was a part, worked till the early hours of the morning to type onto stencils what was a pirated edition of Paulo Freire's classic *Pedagogy of the Oppressed*. By the end of the next day, the first hundred copies of the book had rolled off the cyclostyling machine and were made available to discerning Indian readers. We had got hold of the pirated book from the Philippines, a good many years before the Penguin volume was to appear in the local stores. At the time, Freire's ideas on transformative education and political change made for heady reading, particularly to those who were young, angry, and idealistic. Freire believed that oppressed communities all over the world were caught in the "culture of silence," which made them passive and powerless, unable to "name" their reality, much less change it.

OPPRESSOR AND OPPRESSED— A SIMPLISTIC MODEL

Freire divided social reality after the Marxist manner into "oppressed" and "oppressor." Today, the two-class theory has lost its lustre. Although it is a conceptually useful tool for mobilizing people, it is nevertheless inadequate to understand complex social systems. For example, it has never been able to give a reasonable explanation for caste. What class analysis overlooks are the numerous vertical bonds that integrate people within communities and professions. Take the case of Malaysia, which has three ethnic groups—the Malay, the Chinese, and the Tamils. Although class divisions cut through larger society in Malaysia, most people still see themselves along ethnic and not class lines. They are first and foremost Malay, Chinese, and Tamil. The horizontal divisions of class are neutralized by the vertical bonding of ethnicity. But Freire did make a humane departure from the traditional Marxist paradigm without renouncing its basic thrust: He did not believe that the oppressor had to be destroyed in the process of struggle. The oppressed had an ontological mission to liberate and humanize themselves, and in the process, the oppressor as well. Nor did he feel the need of an all-inclusive party that would speak and act in the place of the people. This allowed for groups and associations to coalesce and empower themselves. His insistence on action that was informed and critiqued by theory, which in turn was tested and corrected by action, was meant to preclude the possibility of dogmas being disguised as truths. But despite his best intentions, his own ideas concealed various forms of dogma, even if they were less menacing than the Marxist–Leninist ones. Freire's emphasis on humanization as the goal of his pedagogy was the most problematic. It completely overlooked the significance of ecological praxis.

This trajectory of action–reflection–action, where the oppressed learned to discern the cause of their oppression and then proceed to change it, was evocatively referred to as *conscientization*. Freire believed that his approach had little to do with spontaneous, unreflected, or dogmatic action. A higher moral purpose was invoked, for conscientization was to be deeply human at the core, with the humanization of social, political, and economic structures as its goal. What made conscientization different from other similar theories was its encapsulation in a method of action that could be understood and practiced by the oppressed themselves. Central to this way of doing things was a mode of literacy where the act of learning to read and write became a process of advancing political awareness. It began by the oppressed forming a "cultural circle" to discuss their problems. In the ensuing discussion, certain words or themes were found to repeat themselves, suggesting that they had impinged deeply into the collective consciousness of the people. These were "generative" words that had the potential to unmask the structures of oppression within a given social situation.

For example, a community might refer to the word *slum* in an uncritical manner. To many of them, a slum could be a place they were condemned to live in because they were uneducated, illiterate, or lazy. Or, expressed in the local idiom, a slum could be a place where a community was living out its karma. Learning to read and write "slum" necessarily led to an extensive discussion on what a slum was, how it was created, and why certain people and not others were obliged to live there. In this process, the community moved from a consciousness that was naive and uncritical to one that was responsible and critical. But an animator who had imbibed Freire's biased worldview usually guided the selection of generative themes. For example, in Indian villages the theme of "earthmother," full of ecological significance, is widely prevalent. Yet the animators would have been reluctant to consider such themes for fear that they might be encouraging superstition.

For Freire, learning to read and write thus becomes a powerful tool to understand the structures of oppression. It leads to action that does not merely provide relief from the symptoms but also tackles the root causes. Freire referred to his method of education as "liberating." It is opposed to the "domesticating" variety, which passively transmits information and condones the situation of oppression. For Freire, education is "the practice of freedom." This is very different from "the fear of freedom" that afflicts the powerless (as well as a lot of us). The fear of freedom may lead a person to see the roles of the oppressor and the oppressed as the only available ones. The conscientization process goes beyond these debilitating choices. To be part of this process implies that education is never neutral. In the process of learning, one is always making choices for something or against something. Above all, education is transforming. It leads to higher forms of consciousness and greater clarity of action.

AN ETHNOCENTRIC WORLDVIEW

Of course, all this implied that people gave up their own worldviews and embraced the one offered by Freire. Although the peoples' world-views may have had traces of fatalism and, in India, hierarchical attitudes of caste, they also carried many values that were important to reconstruct a world that was less oriented toward material progress and development. Freire was not able to see that the dominant notion of progress and development contained within it the seeds of an unsustainable world. If, as a result of the "liberation," the Indian poor eventually attained the standard of living of a middle-class American, the world would be that much nearer ecological collapse. Of course, in the 1970s I was myself an uncritical admirer of Freire and did not see these limitations. I suppose, to be fair to Freire, he had developed his thinking when ecological awareness had not risen to the point it has. Still, Freire's thinking smacks of Western ethnocentrism. By using modern standards related to "progress," he had naively assumed that the thinking of the oppressed was naïve. He had overlooked the fact that the poor refer to the earth as their mother and not as a resource for economic development, that they cultivated the earth organically without chemical fertilizers and pesticides. He had overlooked the fact that tribal and indigenous populations worked through cooperation and consensus rather than aggressive individual competition. But again, this is wisdom I have gained through hindsight. As I said, at the time I was sold on his approach.

I remember the time 25 years ago, when I went to villages around Villupuram, 3 hours from Madras, where young dalits (the name that untouchables have now given themselves) were regularly meeting to understand the ideas of Freire. A few university-educated activists from Madras helped to translate these ideas into Tamil. It was truly a period of hope. In a few months, local struggles against caste oppression began to erupt all over the area. In the years that followed, these ideas spread all over the state. At about the same time, similar movements began to develop all over South India, and shortly thereafter in the north of the country. Freire's books were translated into all the major Indian languages and widely read among social activists.

Things would never be the same for dalits, slum-dwellers, and other excluded communities.

Still, our experience of conscientization work with tribals left us rather anxious in the end. For several years I had interacted closely with the Jenu Kuruba, Betta Kuruba, and Soliga tribes in and around the forest known as the Nagarhole National Park, in Mysore district. Some 25 years ago, a dam was built in the area and the authorities forcibly displaced a large part of the tribal population. In those days there was nobody around to defend their interests. About half the displaced population were given one hectare or so of government wasteland as part of the rehabilitation program. The other half had to fend for themselves. Even those who got land were unable to do much with it. The land was for the most part full of stones and rock, with no water or electricity. For those who did not get land, life was even more precarious. They were left to the mercies of the local landlords or had to manually construct roads for the government, a task they were totally unprepared for. The forest laws got more and more strict for the tribals who remained in the national park. They were not allowed to hunt anymore; cultivating crops became more restricted and cutting wood to build their huts was prohibited. (And now, the government has begun to progressively throw the rest of the tribals out of the forest.)

We started working in this area more than 15 years ago. The task was to build a strong tribal movement that could resist the atrocities committed against them by the forest department, local bureaucrats, and the landlords. We used the consciousness-raising approach advocated by Freire. In addition, modern trade union methods were employed, and in the course of a few years a reasonably strong movement had sprung up. This movement was capable of negotiating with the bureaucrats and forest officials. Many small successes were garnered, like getting back the land, given to them by the government, that the local landlords had earlier expropriated. Or getting bore wells put into some hamlets for drinking water. Or securing old age pensions under a government scheme. It was sometimes even possible to challenge the might of the government, as in the case of a tribal woman who was chased and raped by a forest officer. Normally he would have gotten away with impunity, as this was the done thing. But in this case he was hauled up in court and suspended from service. The case is still going on and the tribal movement is seeking a conviction.

All this work was tenacious and well meaning. But where we had tripped was in the cultural arena. We had assumed we were on the right path. The tribals had to be brought around, through appropriate participatory techniques, to see the rightness of our approach. When the movement was being built, it was discovered that the tribal chiefs were too old-fashioned to understand modern ideas of confrontational politics. After all, the tribals had only known consensual ways of solving conflicts. So we worked with the younger lot and trained them into an activist force. In the bargain, the rug was pulled from under the feet of the chiefs. They lost their authority in the hamlets. With that, the disintegration of a way of life, which had begun with the government throwing them out of the forest, received a further impulse. It was the sanctity of the tribal chief that held the small communities together. Disrespecting them meant weakening the sense of community. The chiefs were certainly disoriented, confused, and unable to discern forces at work. They could not act. But if the movement had dialogued with them, it might have attained some objectives without threatening the internal cohesion of the communities. If we had understood the tribals better, we may have learned a few things from their own consensual way of solving conflicts. As we knew the importance of "cultural action," we taught them revolutionary songs written by nontribal activists from other parts of the state. At the primary schools the children learned these songs. It was only later, perhaps after the damage was done, that we realized that tribals had their own songs, some of which were more appropriate than the ones we brought from outside. It was the same case with stories that were taught to the children. Again, they were stories from outside, including Hans Christian Anderson in translation. There was nothing wrong about learning them, but it was tragic that we were unable to see that stories and fables of the tribals themselves were at least as good as those of Hans Christian Anderson.

Besides the songs and the stories, we had difficulties in knowing what to do with a way of life that seemed significantly superior to the modern, in terms of its underlying values. Tribals believed in

cooperation rather than competition. Their sense of "rights" was community oriented and not individual. They believed that a consensual
approach to problem solving was better than a confrontational one.
They did not plunder the earth and save for the months ahead. They
lived each day as it came, collected food only for the day. If they took
a tuber out of the ground, they let a portion remain to regenerate.
For them the earth was mother. There was no question of speculating
with their mother, of buying and selling her.

So whereas Freire's ideas had played a positive role in enabling
the untouchable dalits to fight caste oppression, the results with
the tribals were disconcerting. It could of course be argued that the
tribals would in any case have been thrown out of the forest by the
government, and that modern values would eventually have pushed
into their universe and unsettled their chiefs. Even if we had not in-
tervened, this might probably have been the outcome. Yet we could
not help feeling that we had contributed to the dismantling of an
ancient way of life, possibly superior in many ways to the one that
modernity has to offer.

THE JEWELLED NET OF INDRA

I last met Paulo Freire about 15 years ago at his modest home in São
Paulo. He was recovering from the depression caused by the death
of his wife Elsa. This did not deter him from a serious, if somewhat
subdued, discussion with me, where he defended the essential ideas
he had nurtured in the past decades. I did not disagree with much of
what he said. However, at one point I suggested that his ideas were
far too influenced by the Enlightenment, which believed in progress
and linear development (even if many referred to the conscientization process as a spiral), where people moved from lower levels of
consciousness to higher ones. Coming from India, I could not deny
that I was at least partially influenced by ideas related to imperma-
nence, to interconnectedness, to the Buddhist notion of the void, to
the significance of the here and now.

I had written an article about the notion of dependent co-arising,
or paticca samuppada, which is central to Buddhism. It suggests

that no one is an island, that we are all "interwoven threads in the intricate tapestry of life." Using the image of the Jeweled Net of Indra to explain these interconnections, the Buddhist writer Joanna Macy (1991) says:

> In the cosmic canopy of Indra's Net, each of us, each jewel at each node of the net, reflects all the others and reflects the others reflecting back. This is what we find when we listen to the sounds of the Earth crying within us—that the tears that arise are not ours alone; they are the tears of an Iraqi mother looking for her children in the rubble; they are the tears of a Navajo uranium miner learning that he is dying of lung cancer. (p. 25)

Interexistence, or interbeing, does not mean that we have no identity, that we are merely part of an undifferentiated whole. What it means is that we are autonomous beings and parts of a larger whole at the same time.

If Freire had listened more closely to the native Indians, he would have been familiar with similar sensibilities. But the *Pedagogy* does not show any familiarity with this important strand in American thinking. More than any other tradition, the thinking of indigenous peoples is permeated with the idea of interconnectedness. Chief Seattle's reflection that "all things are connected" is too well known for me to dwell on here. Another native American, Luther Standing Bear, the Lakota thinker, wrote in 1933, "All this was in accordance with the Lakota belief that man did not occupy a special place in the eyes of Wakan Tanka, the Grandfather of us all. I was only a part of everything that was called world" (1933/1987, p. 42). Commenting on Standing Bear's reflections, John Grim (Bucknell University, USA) states that, "To distinguish the human 'camp' is not an ontological separation of beings, or an ethical judgment about superior and inferior relations between species. To think of human, animal, plant, and mineral bodies as separated by consciousness or personality is a category error" (1983, p. 77). Not only does the human not occupy a special place, but the human is also not separate from the earth and the universe.

I also realized that I was not alone in being sceptical of a model of progress that was based merely on higher levels of consumption, of brutal competition in the market (the dog-eat-dog attitude), of the poisoning of our air, land, and water. It appeared to me that we had placed too much faith in concepts like "progress" and "development" and that political radicalism, while expressing genuine solidarity with the underdog, did not question the basic orientations of the system. Even Marxist theory, in its definition of surplus value, emphasized the role of the working class in its production and overlooked the significance of the resources that the earth provided. Surplus value is not only stolen from the workers, it is also stolen from the earth. Any perspective of liberation that does not critique the fundamental assumptions of the dominant development paradigm ends up being an apology for capitalism. Like Marxism, the Freirean liberative approach, for all its democratic aspirations, also risks ending up as the flip side of capitalism. Any paradigm of transformation, if it is to be sustainable, has to be pro-human and pro-earth at the same time, which means that it must go radically beyond the present left–right dichotomy.

REACHING A PLATEAU

In India, Paulo Freire's contribution to the empowerment of dalits, tribals, and women has been substantial, even if there is little documentation of what happened. The method followed was one of dialogue and confrontation: dialogue within the circles of the oppressed peoples and confrontation against the oppressor. In the process, the freedom of the oppressed communities was enlarged in a limited way. But the enlargement of freedom could go that far and no further. "Limit" situations were reached within a year or two. Most communities achieved a string of victories in the initial period. For example, a dalit community in Tamilnadu was able to force an upper caste landlord to cede a bore well, meant for the whole village, that he had appropriated for himself. Near Mysore, the process led to tribal communities mobilizing to initially defeat a government plan to relocate them outside their traditional forest habitat.

But these early victories eventually led to a plateau without easy exits; the spiral of incremental freedom had reached a premature denouement. In the case of the dalits, they had certainly travelled some way from the feeling that they were a low and impure community who were destined to be the lowest rung of the ladder, at the mercy of upper caste landlords, bureaucrats, and police. They had learned the importance of networking and political mobilization. Socially they could now walk with their heads held a little higher. But economically they were the poorest of the poor and there was little they could do to gain a measure of self-sufficiency, particularly when they did not own some land. Likewise with the tribals, they were so poor (the men earning the equivalent of 50¢ US a day in the early 1990s) that they could not sustain their struggle for too long against a determined government that wanted to displace them from the forest. Besides, the momentum of the struggle had largely disoriented them culturally. Today the displacement process has gone even further and the government is resettling them outside the forest on unfertile land with no water or electricity.

Something else happened in the 1990s that has almost completely transported Freire's ideas to oblivion. This has to do with the end of the Cold War and the collapse of Communism as a workable system. As long as the threat of Communism was real, particularly in Third World contexts, Freire's methods was seen as a soft radical option to stem the tide of Communism. Western donor agencies played an active role in supporting empowerment programs that were based on conscientization, the name given to Freire's method. I do not believe that the employees of donor agencies themselves consciously played this role, but it was a strategy backed by a section of the northern liberal elites. When Communism ceased to be a threat, there was little reason to continue support for these radical alternatives. Other notions like participatory development and civil society took over from conscientization and political mobilization. The donor agencies now faced pressures in their home countries to stop supporting radical programs. From the mid-1990s the rug was pulled from under many a radical NGO. Henceforth they would only receive support for programs that were nonconfrontational, that undertook to create employment skills and implemented projects like microcredit.

JUSTICE: STRUGGLE FOR THE
CONSUMER CAKE?

Since my first encounter with conscientization many years ago, my passion for Freire and his ideas has not abated, although it has necessarily undergone considerable revision. To write this chapter, I searched hard for a copy of the *Pedagogy* and could not find it on my bookshelf or with any of my friends in Bangalore. A few of them had owned more than one copy several years ago but not anymore. It was the same with his second-best-known book, *Cultural Action for Freedom.* I don't know how many copies of the *Pedagogy* I had bought over the years, but there were none left. It was an expensive habit, keeping several copies of a book I liked so that I could give it away to interested friends and activists. All this is to say how times have changed for a thinker that every social activist in India was familiar with in the 1970s and 1980s. I am aware that Freire has now become a big name in the educational departments of many U.S. universities. One could only wish that the more meaningful aspects of Freire's ideas could be incorporated into a holistic perspective that integrates the interdependent nature of reality with a critique of the limitations of the present understandings of social progress. The Freirean method has as much to learn from the traditional wisdom of ordinary peasants as they have to learn from him.

In India today, like much of the world, it is a different intellectual climate altogether where one no longer carries a revered book in the head almost in the manner one carries a mantra. The quest for grand theory is frowned on, and rightly so, although the poorer countries are always susceptible to catch the virus of patchwork efforts to provide their social movements with vision and purpose. Globally, however, the new trends in social theory have done away with the subject, so crucial to Freire. (In the decentring process, so many subjects were apparently discovered that it may well be asked which one Freire was addressing!) Most activists in India are not given to social analysis or critical thinking anymore. It is almost as if we have internalized the social-democratic/liberal political process and do not need to think anymore, as if we have contracted, in the manner of Francis Fukuyama (1992), an ostrich-like "end of history" malaise.

I am aware that the later Paulo Freire has made some clarifications and modifications of his ideas, but I have chosen to remain with the Freire of *Pedagogy of the Oppressed,* his most influential book. Each time I read or teach Freire, I sense a thrill going through me, opening out the pores of my being and urging me to consider that both I and the world can be transformed. As education is not neutral, we are either making the journey to fullfilment or going the other way. Each time I hear this notion, I am awakened to the possibilities in myself, even if I am not always clear if it is as simple as it seems for a community that is oppressed. Education is certainly the practice of freedom but a freedom that is circumscribed by the hidden hand of a system where both oppressed and oppressors are victims, even if the oppressed experience a double oppression: excluded from the bare necessities of survival on one hand and partially impacted by fantasies spawned by advertising and marketing industries on the other. But when Freire insists that the vocation of man is to be fully human, I suddenly break out of my excitement and see with dismay the completely anthropocentric nature of his endeavor. Freire fails to see that the goal of humanization leads us away from the interconnectedness we experience with all living beings and the earth.

Up to the 1960s and 1970s, the struggle was seen in Left and Right terms. It had to do with the division of the cake. The right wanted to appropriate as much of the cake as possible for itself, whereas the left wanted it distributed to the greatest number. But few had pondered on the worthiness of the cake itself. Today we know that the cake has environmental maggots inside and that the icing is laced with pesticides. We also know that the bigger the cake gets, the more likely we will ecologically self-destruct. But the push for the unsustainable cake keeps getting stronger and stronger, fed by the relentless need of the market to grow bigger and bigger, seducing humans with more and more needs. Mohandas Gandhi, who was an early critic of industrial progress, was a fervent advocate of simple living. He believed that "the distinguishing characteristic of modern civilization is an indefinite multiplication of wants" (1954, p. 35). His own physical needs were limited, subsisting on simple vegetarian food and goats' milk and manually spinning his yarn. His mud hut in his ashram at Wardha is a constant reminder of how little one needs to live gracefully and joyfully. Gandhi (1954) fought against poverty, but revelled in simplicity. He was convinced that "the world has enough for everybody's need, but not enough for one person's greed" (p. 52). Today, consumerism has not only legitimized greed but also multiplied needs. People of all classes are becoming victims of the grand delusion that a market-driven society is projecting with the active complicity of the media. The cake is getting bigger and more extravagant, even if many people are excluded from its taste or experience it only vicariously. Not only are democracies becoming plutocracies and social justice becoming a distant dream, we are also in danger of destroying our life-support systems by lethally damaging our environment and bleeding mother earth. The answer lies in developing paradigms of simple living as alternatives to unsustainable consumerism.

INTERBEING:
AN INNER–OUTER PRAXIS

But how do we get there? The metaphor of Indra's net, where we are all interconnected and interdependent, could serve as a guiding vision to steer us away from the notion of the separate individual, lonely to the core, who has to compete from birth to death in a world propelled by money. The Gandhian synthesis of spirituality and politics can also offer insights to restart the stalled, and flawed, spiral of Freire. Gandhi's spirituality was as transparent as his politics. He meditated, fasted, and prayed in the thick of turbulent politics. It seemed to give him courage, compassion, and clarity. Not only that, it powerfully connected him to millions of illiterate people in India. A spiritual field was in place that enabled people to persist even if the results were uncertain. Gandhi believed in the Bhagvat Gita ideal of Nishkama Karma, that one had to act without expecting the fruits of one's action. One acted because it was right to do so, and not because one expected to see the results in one's lifetime. In times such as ours, we need the strength to sustain many actions whose results may never see the light of day in our lifetime.

In the summer of 1989, Raimundo Pannikar and I met in Paris at the house of Marc Levy, a Jewish friend who was an astute observer of political events in France. Pannikar was nattily dressed in a tea-colored suit and a silk scarf, every inch a ladies' man. The conversation that evening veered round to the role of conflict in the resolution of problems. At the time, I coordinated an institute in Paris, founded by Paulo Freire and Collette Humbert, that was concerned with studying social movements. I was half-convinced (in politics, I am rarely convinced all the way) of the importance of dialectics in promoting social change. A landlord and a tenant had to clash for the just resolution of the problem of landlessness. Likewise, one idea clashed with another to produce a superior idea; put differently, thesis and antithesis had to cross swords for a new synthesis to emerge. This was dialectics, the way progress was made, how history charted its course. Panikkar disagreed with me. He believed in dialogue, in the Chinese notion of yin–yang, where reality was not divided into polar opposites, where the yin contained the yang and the yang the yin. Panikkar believed neither in reform nor revolution. For him revolution was only "deformation." He preferred something more radical, what he called *transformation*. Transformation was the result of dialogue, not dialectics.

Gandhi was a critical traditionalist who was wary of modernity. He saw industrial civilization as violent, competitive, and destructive of nature. Freire's approach draws from modern sources like Karl Marx and Frantz Fanon, emphasizing the essential goodness of scientific progress, provided the fruits are justly managed and distributed. "Critical consciousness" was totally modern in the way he conceived it. I must admit I have always been a little uncomfortable with his enthusiasm to move people from their "naïve" consciousness to a critical one. Granted, people can be apathetic and naïve when they face oppression. But, as I stated earlier, Freire does not adequately appreciate that these very same people are naïve about some things and clear about others. Apart from being street smart, they are also storehouses of traditional wisdom related to health, agriculture, and technology. They are reservoirs of psychological and spiritual energy, which could serve to sustain alternate paradigms. For example, traditional Hindu spirituality has given little priority to competitive and material goals. Buddhism believes that nothing is permanent and that the cause of human suffering is to cling to things believing they are permanent. Therefore consumerism, which is concerned with possessing and gratifying the senses, would go counter to the more meaningful strains of Buddhism and Hinduism. Gandhi himself, as a young man, went about imitating Western manners and behavior, even going to the extent of taking dancing lessons. But he did not get far with his uncritical emulation of the English. He soon realized that his strengths actually lay hidden within him and that it did not matter if he was a poor speaker or was frail-looking. He converted his inner spiritual and psychological strengths into a powerful energy for political transformation. I have always been intrigued at India's inability to win a single Olympic gold medal in athletics. I think that competition in sports is not part of our culture. It has been suggested that our strengths lay elsewhere, in the realm of the spirit (although India has sadly lost much of this spirit in recent decades). That is why a nation of one billion people has been unable to win a single gold medal in the Olympics—apart from one medal in hockey several decades ago when, other than Pakistan, few nations took the game seriously.

Post-modernism has robbed us of the subject. But the presence of multiple subjectivities should not deter us from acknowledging the existence of another kind of subject, which I call the *deep subject*. This deep subject is *interbeing*, not a separate reality. It is a node in Indra's net. It derives its sustenance and identity from its interconnectedness with all other humans and the natural world. This deep subject needs to be acknowledged, nurtured, and enlisted into the spiral of praxis for its potential to enable us to progressively deepen our connections with each other, the earth, and the cosmos. It is not an instrumentality but an energy that gives us purpose and coherence, that transforms history even while it is transhistorical. This is, of course, a far cry from Freire's unsatisfactory notion of humanization. In fact, it can be argued that when the human is seen as "separate," it inevitably leads to suffering, oppression, and ecological disaster.

Today the oppressed and the oppressor are subject to the machinations of the culture of instant gratification, which are peddled by the market and communicated through the advertising and marketing industries. At this point in time, perhaps only the deep subject can help us discern what may genuinely lead us to interexistence and what may not. The metaphor of the bow and arrow may help clarify further. The arrow shoots outward and finds its mark only when it is drawn inward in the bow. This is a self-evident principle. But what of arrows that shoot out without being drawn inward? Obviously they are illusions and not real ones. Our virtual and consumer society is concerned with despatching illusory arrows that cannot find their mark, for they are not real arrows to begin with. Our political convictions and our desire to change ourselves are lacking in substance because they have not been drawn inward in the psychospiritual bow. And as there is no inward journey, there can be no outward journey. An outer praxis without an inner praxis lacks conviction. Genuine critical awareness and transformation entails changing social and ecological practice as well as the deep structures of our consciousness. Liberation is as much an inner as an outer event.

In the end, we can save the earth only if we believe it is sacred. Our universe began 15 billion years ago with the Big Bang. The earth has been around for about 4.6 billion years. It took a long time for the earth to cool and give birth to life. The first single-celled organism came into being only about 1.5 billion years ago. This organism differentiated, became more and more complex, and finally produced our ancestors a few hundred thousand years ago. So, scientifically speaking, it is the earth that has given birth to all life. The earth is our first mother and is deserving of all the honor and respect we accord a mother. Our connectedness with the earth must be the cornerstone of any significant approach to political liberation. The energy field that connects the earth to us is the ground of our being, the spirit that flows through all matter. This same spirit points to another conception of the good life, which has less to do with accumulating consumer goods and more to do with the celebration of nature, our inner spaces, and our friendships. Only such a deep conviction of interbeing (which I have elsewhere referred to as *earth spirituality*) can enable us to be considerate to other human beings and prevent us from destroying our life-support systems through the mindless pollution of air, water, and earth.

REFERENCES

Gandhi, M. (1954). *Autobiography: The story of my experiments with truth.* Washington, DC: Washington Public Affairs Press.

Grim, J. A. (1983). *The shaman: Patterns of Siberian and Ojibway healing.* Norman, OK: University of Oklahoma Press.

Fukuyama, F. (1992). *The end of history and the last man.* New York: The Free Press.

Luther Standing Bear. (1987). *Land of the Spotted Eagle.* Chicago: Loyola University Press. (Original work published 1933)

Macy, J. (1991). *Mutual causality in Buddhism and general systems theory: The dharma of natural systems.* Albany, NY: State University of New York Press.

6

Whose Oppression Is This? The Cultivation of Compassionate Action in Dissolving the Dualistic Barrier

Phyllis Robinson

FREIRE AND WHO?

I remember my first glimpse of Paulo Freire's *Pedagogy of the Oppressed*. It was as I prepared for entrance into a graduate program where Freire's philosophy and methods were considered sacrosanct. I was beginning graduate school just after spending 7 years living and practicing in Zen centers. Bestowed with the blessings of my Buddhist teachers, I was compelled to take a fragile open-heartedness out into the world of suffering beings. In my desire for a livelihood that would complement a yearning to do service, I sought a profession in which I could engage in compassionate social action. A university program with Freire at its inspirational helm seemed to present a means to fulfill this avocational longing.

This essay describes a personal journey. Contained within the tes-
timonial are the meanderings of a person brimming with good intentions and a wisdom eye not fully opened. The story is told as the teller
matured on the spiritual path. There is a noticeable and gradual shift
in the author as she moves from believing in ideals to discovering the
wisdom that emerges from experience. She learns that seeking truth
about knowledge and power involves holding, moment to moment, a
series of open questions: What is the nature of the knower? What is
the nature of that which is known? What is the nature of the relationship between the two? These are both epistemological and spiritual
questions. They are central to this storyteller's experience in her years
of attempting to apply Freire's pedagogy in service to the struggle of
the Cambodian people. Cambodian friends and colleagues became
the author's teachers as, despite her interventions, they sought to
reclaim their dignity, their homes, their livelihood, and their families
after two and half decades of displacement and civil war.

WHO OR WHAT IS BEING LIBERATED?

Let us return to this first encounter with Freire's theory of oppression. I remember an initial feeling of strong respect for his obvious
and profound love for humankind. There was also puzzlement as
I realized that there might be inconsistency on two levels with my
Zen experience. The first was with Freire's view of oppression and
liberation. They seemed limited to the relative plane of existence
that, from a Buddhist practitioner's standpoint, is inseparable from
the absolute plane of existence. To limit liberation to the realization
of critical consciousness, which is an activity of the thinking mind,
did not venture deep enough into what I had just begun to understand through meditation practice about the internal causes of our
imprisonment. In my limited experience, our imprisonment appeared
to stem ultimately from an attachment to the illusion of some solid
permanent entity called a *self*. Each time I returned to the breath during practice, labeling my thoughts "thinking," it became clearer how
this illusory self is constructed thought by thought. If one is liberated

only at the level of thought, then what lies unexamined beneath it all? The potential would exist, even after critical consciousness had been achieved, that there would remain a blind spot of ignorance. From this ignorance, the critically aware would continue to be imprisoned in a fearful quest to protect and perpetuate a self that does not actually exist. Out of ignorance, the now confident and supposedly empowered ego would predictably visit its new-found powers on others, contributing to the cycles of human suffering.

The second limitation I found stemmed from the fact of there having to be someone who knows about oppression and those who are oppressed. Even though the means by which these two beings come together is in dialogue and Freire himself refers to dialogue as "an act of love," from a Buddhist practitioner's standpoint true compassion is nondualistic. In the Zen Center I had been presented with the teachings of Zen Masters who had had the direct realization of the illusion of self. For them, the illusory barriers between self and others—self and the world—had fallen away. At this point compassion became manifest in selfless service. One such teacher, Zen Master Dogen Kigen (1200–1253), presented liberation as already our natural state, hidden from us through a persistent clinging to the solidity of existence—fueled paradoxically by a fear that we may not exist.

As profound as that might sound, I was about to enter a graduate program lacking confidence that my experience on the meditation cushion and the inspiration of my Zen ancestors was sufficient to steer my course through the world of concepts and theories about oppression and liberation. Little did I know the ways in which this illusory ego/self would manifest as I sought to link my educational training for a livelihood with the Buddhist teachings on compassion and action.

PRAXIS AND PARADOX

From 1989 to 1997, I was both a masters and eventually a doctoral student in a program housed within the School of Education at the University of Massachusetts called the Center for International Education (CIE). In our field of participatory adult and nonformal education and research, Paulo Freire was presented by our faculty as one among many of our program's inspirational leaders. The professors' teaching style, the classroom, and overall program structures at CIE were experiential models for participatory learning. As graduate students, we were encouraged to navigate the intricate web of theories surrounding knowledge and power. As "deep practitioners," we were expected to work from within a dialectic of theory and practice and to use this praxis-based approach in the geographical circularity of field work in adult education and the university classroom. My own field work while a graduate student was primarily with Cambodian women in a variety of domestic and overseas settings.

THE THAI–CAMBODIAN BORDER

It was 1992. I had just received a grant to develop a participatory educational experience on traditional and nontraditional approaches to mental health to be carried out in a month-long workshop in a refugee camp on the Thai–Cambodian border. The World Federation of Mental Health had done a comprehensive survey in the camps in 1991 and had determined that a large percentage of the camp population was suffering from depression or suicidal tendencies. It did not take The World Federation of Mental Health to know that this was a result of the multiple traumas of displacement, war, and attempted genocide—to say nothing of living in refugee camps for 10 years or more.

A Cambodian-American colleague and I spent one month in the Site Two camp prior to the workshop, conducting a feasibility study. Site Two was the temporary home of 179,000 displaced Cambodians. We interviewed nuns, monks, lay leaders, and nongovernment organization staff. We determined that a self-selected group of Cambodian Buddhist nuns, who practiced meditation and were already giving informal advice to troubled women, could be matched with a group of young Cambodian women who were currently receiving training in Western counseling techniques and that both parties could mutually benefit from exposure to one another's knowledge. Both the nuns in the camp temples and the young women who were being trained as counselors in Western-style approaches were already or soon would be called on to minister to the needs of the troubled families, especially the women, who, with their children, comprised 80% of the camp population.

Although in our preconceived plan both the nuns and the young women would mutually learn from each other, in the actual workshop, the nuns were very reluctant to speak up in the sharing sessions. I asked my colleague to ask them to teach their meditation techniques and to speak of Buddhist principles of healing for the benefit of the younger women. When pressed for a reason for their silence, they informed me through the translator that knowledge is a gift given to some based on merit-making in past lives. According to their belief system, if one has knowledge, it is as a result of previous good deeds from other lifetimes, thus explaining one's current role as one who possesses knowledge or one who does not. I see now how incredulous it was to assume that their current knowledge was worthwhile simply because I came in and told them so.

I remember returning from the field setting and reading anthropologists Geertz's (1976) and Ledgerwood's (1990) claims that in Southeast Asia this kind of thinking is based on a complicated hierarchical epistemological system that combines Brahminism and Buddhist karmic principles. The nuns believed that they were born into this lifetime with past karma requiring them to be of service to monks. Through selfless service (merit-making), there would be a better chance in the next life to perhaps be the one who is the possessor of knowledge. It was true. The nuns had always deferred speaking about any topic such as meditation to a higher authority, namely their meditation teacher or a monk. I now began to realize why my Cambodian-American colleague had been so upset with my badgering her to create an environment for the nuns to share their knowledge. During our planning sessions in the hotel each night, she would tell me, in a polite manner, that my insisting that she maintain a participatory educational environment was inappropriate. I simply could not accept it, and took a strong stance that we maintain a vigilance in favor of participatory methodologies.

After returning to the university, I persisted in the belief that these women had been oppressed by their religion. I set up interviews with Cambodian monks in my community, inquiring as to the reasons why the nuns would have no sense of the value of their own knowledge. My conclusions from these conversations were that Buddhist monks in Southeast Asian countries have, through the ages, interpreted the dying out of the female monastic tradition 2000 years prior (supposedly predicted by the Buddha) as a reason not to support the education of nuns. These discoveries fueled my adherence to a critical theoretical position. I then felt it necessary to convince my Cambodian-American colleague that, through providing a participatory environment, the nuns would have eventually gained self-confidence about the value of their knowledge. Ideally, once the nuns returned to their country, that we needed to encourage the Buddhist hierarchy in Cambodia to provide equal educational opportunities for nuns. I wrote these arguments into a draft of my Masters thesis in which I explored Freire's stages of consciousness as it applied to the Cambodian nuns. In this exploration, I explained that the nuns' worldview was both magical and naive. They were functioning completely out of a sense of security in their belief that they had no control over their world and were victims of karmic cycles from many past lives. They had accepted their fate as "the one in society who defers to those who have had a better karmic proclivity to know." I told my colleague that this was left over from Brahmanism and had nothing to do with Buddhism. The Buddha, in fact, defied the caste system in India and insisted that all beings were equally capable of achieving enlightenment. What needed to be lifted, I told her, were the veils of ignorance. I finally sent this tirade of words off in the mail and asked for her comments. She wrote back furious. She called me many names, including ethnocentric. Her criticism was scathing and defensive. One particular comment stands out among the others. She reminded me that Cambodian nuns are traditionally not engaged in the practice of building up their sense of confidence in a self, but in dissolving ego attachment.

THE CONCEPTUAL SOLACE
OF POST-MODERNISM

One of the great gifts of the human spirit is the ability to transform suffering so that adversity becomes a force that awakens us. Rather than being overpowered by forces of confusion or despair, we can begin to see that we have a choice in how we let ourselves be affected, that we're not entirely helpless in the face of adversity. (Bennett-Goleman, 2001, p. 294)

In the Vajrayana practice of Tibetan Buddhism (of which I am now a student), it is said that within the very moment when the rug is pulled out, there lies a great opportunity. This moment of groundlessness can cause us to wake up. When we actually experience what my current Buddhist teacher, Pema Chodron, calls "the big squeeze"—the moment when our ideals and the reality of what is really happening do not match up—it is considered one of the most productive places on the spiritual path. It was a challenge to let go into the groundlessness of what was laid before me by the circumstances of my Cambodian ex-friend's attack. I did allow the pain of her rejection to help me release my attachment to the belief that participatory education and Freire's pedagogy and theories were universally applicable.

As I prepared my Masters thesis, I sought conceptual solace in the post-modern language of deconstruction. The writings, particularly those of post-modern men such as Jacques Derrida, Michel Foucault, and Richard Rorty, represented theories (even critical theories) as discourses, constructed realities based on and motivated by the maintenance of the power of a particular knowledge system. A knowledge system, in this case, whose raison d'etre was in response to premodern atrocities (the burning of witches and the drawing and quartering of heretics). Our modern way of knowing had emerged to protect those in Europe and eventually in America from the darkest of ages. It was the principles of the Enlightenment and the epistemology that followed in its ethical wake that has shaped our universal doctrine of human rights (to say nothing of our present-day academic system). Our current view of social justice (and this is why Freire's pedagogy was such a welcomed approach) is based on the assumption of a universal ideal of knowledge equity—all beings as individuals have the right to equal access to education and the ability to be freed of authoritarian systems that would deny them that access. A pedagogy that provided those being denied this access with tools of both political awareness and self-awareness of their own collusion in the perpetuation of this system of oppression is a seductive pedagogy indeed—especially for those of us who thought we could "save the world" by becoming experts of oppression.

In my fervor to address suffering in its myriad forms, I had failed to examine whether critical theory and the pedagogy of the oppressed were self-reflexive (exhibiting awareness of the epistemological assumptions underlying its theory and ideals). I was now able, with experience as my guide, to revisit the place at the beginning of this chapter when I described my first reading of Freire and had, at the time, an insight (only partially grounded in experience) that his theory of oppression ignored the possibility of an emancipatory theoretician and agent having a constructed self. Both the post-structuralists and post-modernists helped me to see how my seduction by the theories of oppression were married to an assumption. This assumption was that Frerie's pedagogy and the critical theories that are the foundation of participatory methodologies, the support of a universal doctrine of human (women's) rights, and even aspects of promoting democracy and civil society were neutral-ground-levelers in the playing field of social justice. As post-modernism and post-structuralism so aptly pointed out, these values I have held so dear were actually born of and limited by the language and sensibilities of my, Freire's, and the critical theorists' conditioning in the ideals of the Enlightenment and Western rationalism. It was important to discover at this point that not everyone on the planet places the individual rights of human beings above or distinct from spirit, nature, and community, and that some peoples of the world live their lives with the understanding that the nature of existence is based on principles of hierarchical association which, when respected and understood, can result in harmonious societal relationships. I also realized that my belief that the world is out there and pregiven, and that I could therefore fix it, was situated in my Western historical conditioning as well.

Discourse, deconstruction, and nonfoundational reality all seemed a good fit for the Buddhist teachings on the constructed self that I had long ago set aside in my fervor to fix the world. I went on to write my doctoral thesis raising the question, "Whose oppression is this?" and feeling, in my discovery of post-modernism, that I had returned home. Yet, I felt befuddled by the relativism that would rip away any project to address social injustice, whatsoever. I still believed that my understanding of the Cambodian nuns oppression was partially accurate. Yet I knew that some part of me would never comprehend how different our worldviews were and therefore how presumptuous it was of me to think that I could aid in the dissolution of the outward manifestation of what I saw as their imprisonment.

THIRD WORLD AND WOMEN-OF-COLOR FEMINISM

About this time, women of color and Third World women had found their voice in deconstructing the Western liberal feminist project. Cultural feminists, Islamic feminists, Black feminists, and others greatly enhanced my understanding of the multiplicity of women's experience. The multiplicity of social identity had nullified my idea of a universal "we." Pluralism was a welcomed antidote to any singular idea of what women's oppression looks like across race, class, and nationality. In addition, monolithic frames of analysis seemed to deny Third World women their sociohistorical uniqueness. This was speaking to my direct experience of the Cambodian nuns.

POST-MODERN AND POST-STRUCTURAL FEMINISM

In response, I read of Western feminists expressing fear that post-modernism would stymie action of any kind on behalf of humankind. This was a period of exploration and retrenchment as Western feminists realized the serious political consequences that the rejection of emancipatory theory might have on all marginalized groups. Post-structural feminists Carmen Luke and Jennifer Gore actually found parallels between feminist thought and post-modernism. I found their explorations courageous. In their willingness to be self-aware, Luke (1992) states that "post-structural feminist epistemology accepts that knowledge is always provisional, open-ended and relational" (p. 27). A post-structural feminist educator, Patti Lather (1991), attempted

in her book, *Getting Smart*, to suggest ways to achieve a liberatory
practice without a liberatory intent. She spoke of a need to search
for ways "to treat our thoughts not as a system, but as a relationship."
Lather also suggested a way in which we can acknowledge our position as social actors in history within an unfixed position in which:

> The goal is a shift from the romantic view of the self as an unchang-
> ing, authentic essence to a concept of self as a conjunction of diverse
> social practices produced and positioned socially without an underly-
> ing essence. (1991, p. 82)

I remember wondering if Lather was speaking here from the wisdom
of a meditation practice. Even though what she was saying appeared
to expound the realization of a constructed self, plus she had coupled
this realization with a nonattached yearning to be of service in an
unjust world, I wondered if in order to accomplish this "shift from a
romantic view of the self" one might need to move beyond a simple
conceptual commitment of seeing the self in this way. It had been
my direct experience that in order to recognize the constructed self,
acknowledging its illusory nature, and to then be able to let go of it
over and over in repeated acts of selfless service to others requires a
disciplined ongoing practice of some kind.

A PEDAGOGY OF THE OPPRESSOR

At this juncture of my unfolding journey, the focus of the oppression
shifted. Suddenly I saw the need for a pedagogy of the oppression
expert. My colleague, Derek Rasmussen, examines this same premise
with a slightly different twist in chapter 7 of this book. I offer, in
the concluding section of this chapter, some insights into what a
pedagogy for the oppression expert might look like. Combining post-
modern deconstruction (as already described) and the ancient Buddhist practice of mindfulness, I challenge the reader to imagine how
an ongoing realization of a constructed self can begin to dissolve the
separation of the oppressed and the one who knows about oppression—moving from dualism to nondualism, from the objectification
of truth as something "out there" to discover, to a mutual discovery

of multiple truths infused with the knowledge of our own cultural conditioning and the wisdom and compassion that can accompany this realization in service to all beings.

I also invite the reader to examine his or her resistance to this approach simply because it has been named as a "Buddhist" practice. Even though it is a 2,500-year-old practice that owes its authorship to a historical figure known as Buddha or "awakened one," one does not have to be or become a Buddhist to practice mindfulness. It is simply a pathway that illuminates the potentiality for human transformation beyond the nihilism expounded in post-modern deconstruction. It helps us see the conditioning of our minds in a moment-to-moment way and it starts right here, right now in this very body, in this very mind.

COMPASSIONATE WORLDS
WITHOUT GROUND

When we are able to be there without saying "I certainly agree with this," or "I definitely agree with that," but just be there directly, then we find fundamental richness everywhere. It is not ours or theirs but is available always to everyone. (Chodron, 1997, p. 101)

This is not the time or the place to go deeply into the mindfulness practice or to discuss groundlessness conceptually. However, in simple terms, the Buddha taught that there is a direct link between our ability to be compassionate and the clarity of our own mind. The barrier I experienced again and again in the work I have described with the nuns and with Freire's pedagogy, and the ideal of knowledge equity through participatory methods, was attachment to view. How does attachment arise? In Buddhist terms it is said that attachment comes when we believe that the self is a solid and fixed entity. All of our thoughts, concepts, and ideals aid in the creation of this solid sense of self:

The mindfulness/awareness student first begins in meditation by observing, in a precisely prescribed fashion, what the mind is doing, its restless, perpetual, grasping, from moment to moment. This beginning enables the student to free oneself from some of one's habitual

patterns of thought, which leads to further mindfulness. Eventually
we begin to realize that there is no self in any of our actual experiences. This discovery can be disturbing. It can cause the student to
lose heart and tempt one to swing to the other extreme, that of nihilism. This flight into nihilism demonstrates that the reflex to cling to a
substantial self is so strong and deep-seated that we reify its absence
as a sort of abyss.

As the student-practitioner continues, however, and as the mind
relaxes further into awareness, a sense of warmth and inclusiveness begins to appear quite naturally. The mentality of watchful self-interest
slips away gradually to be replaced by a natural interest in others. The
conscious realization of the sense of relatedness and the development
of a more impartial sense of warmth is experienced. It is what is referred to as "karuna" or compassion (Varela, 1992, pp. 68–69).

I subtitled this chapter *The Cultivation of Compassionate Action in
Dissolving the Dualistic Barrier*. The attachment of ego to any theory
or ideal, in this case as it relates to social justice, creates a barrier. You
are oppressed and I am the one who knows about your oppression.
This is the dualistic barrier. This results from having been conditioned
by our senses to believe that we are separate agents from those we
help and from the world. (It is also as a result of our historical conditioning in the values of the Enlightenment, which deconstruction
addresses.) Because of our senses of sight, sound, smell, taste, touch,
and mind, we experience the world naturally as dualistic. Nondualism and the natural compassion that arises from it are not ideals to
strive toward. In fact, they are pure conjecture until we actually have
a direct experience and even then the mind naturally wants to grasp
this experience and make it permanent. The Buddhist teachings have
never asked the practitioner to take things on faith but to practice
meditation in order to have a gradual and direct understanding of the
constructed nature of self. When we begin to see the illusory nature
of the constructed self, it becomes possible to let go. We let go over
and over again over the course of a lifetime. Why? Because living
in the world of the senses and the world of concepts, the self wants
to continually reconstruct itself. Mindfulness is therefore not just a
technique, it is a way of life. And there may come, at some point,
the experience of oneness with all things. With this realization, we

begin to live our lives knowing that the world is not out there to be managed or manipulated. Phenomenon arises and we are in a state of readiness to meet it.

Living and working in ways that acknowledge service to those who suffer also means coming to know deeply the nature of our own suffering. Chodron (1997) puts it very clearly:

> Compassionate action is an incredibly difficult way of working with human beings. It means not shutting down on that which challenges our beliefs. It means first of all not shutting down on ourselves. This means allowing ourselves to feel what we feel and not pushing it away. It means accepting every aspect of ourselves, even the parts we don't like. Only in an open non-judgmental space can we acknowledge what we are feeling. Only in an open space where we're not all caught up in our own version of reality can we see and hear and feel who others really are, which allow us to be with them and communicate with them properly. (pp. 78–79)

I know that I am not alone when I say that there are many old wounds that still manifest in my relationships in the world. For this reason, I combine mindfulness practice with a form of loving kindness or metameditation. This helps set the tone of opening to the pain, the blame, the self-denigration that accompany things falling apart. Loving kindness practice says that it is all embraceable. Nothing is outside of the sacred circle. Daily practice has slowly begun the flowering within of an unconditional friendliness toward all of my states of mind and even in loosening the grasping of these states of mind as mine. When I remember to do it, it allows me to begin each day with an embracing quality of mind. The inner battlefield dissipates in the decision to bring mindfulness to my busy, opinionated mind, my self-negating mind, the mind that does not think I'm good enough. And that too and that too and that too—nothing is left out of the unconditioned embrace, the realization of basic goodness, the letting go of ego, breath by breath, moment by moment.

There is a final quote I would like to end with:

> Serving requires me to know that my humanity is more powerful than my expertise. What is most professional is not always what best serves and strengthens the wholeness in others. Fixing and helping create a

distance between people. . . . I cannot serve at a distance. I can only
serve that to which I am profoundly connected, that which I am willing to touch. Fixing and helping are strategies to repair life. I serve life
not because it is broken but because it is holy. (Remen, 1999, p. 25)

REFERENCES

Bennett-Goleman, T. (2001). *Emotional alchemy: How the mind can heal the heart.*
New York: Random House.
Chodron, P. (1997). *When things fall apart: Heart advice for difficult times.* Boston,
MA: Shambhala Publications.
Freire, P. (1990). *Pedagogy of the oppressed* (Rev. ed.). New York: Continuum.
Geertz, C. (1976). *Interpretations of culture.* New York: Basic Books.
Lather, P. (1991). *Getting smart.* New York and London: Routledge.
Ledgerwood, J. (1990). *Changing Khmer conceptions of gender: Women, stories and the
social order.* Dissertation Abstracts International, 42, Microfilms # 7721750.
Luke, C. (1992). Feminist politics in radical pedagogy. In C. Luke & J. Gore (Eds.),
Feminism and critical pedagogy (pp. 25–53). New York: Routledge.
Remen, N. R. (1999, September). Helping, fixing or serving? *The Shambhala Sun,*
25–27.
Varela, F. J. (1992). *Ethical know-how: Action, wisdom and cognition.* Palo Alto, CA:
Stanford University Press.

7

Cease to Do Evil, *Then* Learn to Do Good ... (A Pedagogy for the Oppressor)

Derek Rasmussen

In Inuit culture our elders are our source of wisdom. They have a long-term view of things and a deep understanding of the cycles and changes of life. . . . So it was natural for us to respect the newcomers who seemed to know how to survive and how to make their organizations work. Their power looked like wisdom. . . . We now know that it [was] a mistake. . . .

Our people did not have any institutional immunity, just as we had no immunity to measles or alcohol. When these institutions came into our lives we had no way to deal with their poisonous side effects, their tendency to undermine wisdom, and our spirits slowly began to die. In our weakened condition we attracted even more services and more rescuers, and the cycle got worse.

—Nunavik Educational Task Force
(1992, pp. 11–13)

> Freire's view that there are "powerless" populations is,
> on anthropological grounds, highly questionable. . . .
> Freirean and other participatory activists have tended
> to disvalue traditional and vernacular forms of power
> . . . because their understanding of power is largely de-
> rived from European Leftist traditions. . . . In short, the
> inappropriate imposition of a certain vision of power
> on people who may not perceive themselves as power-
> less and, moreover, may not want to be empowered in
> the way being prescribed, is a problem area that has
> not been sufficiently addressed by Freireans. Nowhere
> is this more evident than Freire's failure to address
> the possibility that educators may be unable (or even
> unwilling) to strangle the oppressor within them. . . .
> The greatest danger of Freire's pedagogy, it would thus
> appear, is that it can be used as a very subtle Trojan
> Horse, one which appears to be a gift to the poor, but
> can all too easily contain a hidden agenda.
> —Blackburn (2000, p. 13)

THE RESCUERS

Paulo Freire was a "Rescuer." Rescuers attempt to ameliorate conditions of the oppressed (certainly a worthy aim); however, rescuers
seem oblivious to the possibility of stemming the oppression of others
in the first place.

One of the facts essential to decoding the rescuer mythology is
the understanding that 20% of the world's people living in affluence
consume 80% of the world's resources; "the remaining 4.7 billion
people—80% of the population—survive on less than a quarter of
world output" (Wackernagel & Rees, 1995, p. 102). Taking 80% of
other folks' stuff does not seem to me to be very neighborly. Rushing
next door after the fact to see if you can help seems the height of
effrontery. It is a young Euro-American civilization that presumes
upon itself the mission of rescuing the rest of the world, when, in
fact, the rest of the world tends to view Euro-America as the culprit

who threw them overboard to start with. Witness Lawrence Harrison, senior fellow at Harvard, reciting a familiar tune when he argues that "culture is the obstacle"' to development in Latin America; therefore, American "social scientists" must find "ways to actively change cultural values in underdeveloped countries." "The problem is culture, and the solution is to change it in the countries where it is impeding prosperity" (quoted in Barss, 2000, p. A15). Harrison's remarks echo those of *The Economic Journal*, which, 40 years earlier in a moment of astonishing honesty, described the development-rescue-mission as follows:

> Economic development of an underdeveloped people by themselves is not compatible with the maintenance of their traditional customs and mores. . . . What is needed is a revolution in the totality of social, cultural and religious institutions and habits, and thus in their psychological attitude, their philosophy and way of life. What is therefore required amounts in reality to social disorganization. Unhappiness and discontent in the sense of wanting more than is obtainable at any moment is to be generated. The suffering and dislocation that may be caused in the process may be objectionable, but it appears to be the price that has to be paid for economic development; the condition for economic progress. (Griffin, 1995, p. 133)

Already, over 100 years ago, "about 85% of the land mass of the earth was either a colony of Europe or a former colony of Europe,"[1] their resources being diverted to what Winston Churchill (1951) would later call "the rich men dwelling at peace within their habitations" (p. 382).

As Kloppenburg (1991) noted, "Indigenous people have in effect been engaged in a massive program of foreign aid to the urban populations of the industrialized North" (p. 16). One present-day South American Indian leader refers to this as the "Marshalltezuma Plan," and has written to European governments asking that they repay the gold and silver borrowed between 1503 and 1660, arguing that Friedman has been proven correct: "A subsidized economy can never function properly, and [this] compels us to claim—for their

---

[1] Dion-Buffalo and Mohawk (1994), "Thoughts from an Autochthonous Center." *Cultural Survival Quarterly*, Winter, p. 33.

own good—the repayment of capital and interest which we have so generously delayed all these centuries" (Cuautemoc, 1998, p. 34).

To mature cultures, the resources that Euro-America gobbles up are interwoven necessities of land and life; they have been uprooted and dissolved in order for our economy to make use of them. We dissolve so that we can buy and sell the pieces. Lohman describes colonialism and development as the processes that "break down" the "social universe" of "partly independent wholes—cultures, languages, practices of livelihood, theories, arts, sciences," and "uses the fragments, deprived of their old roles, to build up new wholes of potentially global scope":

> Farmland and forests have been removed from local fabrics of subsistence and converted to substrates for export cropping; rivers usurped to provide power for new urban sectors. . . . The diversity of knowledge held by local people has been devalued, pulverized and supplanted by a handful of disciplines—Western science, economics and management—controlled by outsiders. . . . Cultural characteristics like family loyalty, proficiency in traditional medicine, or patron–clientage, meanwhile, become sources of "comparative advantage" to be exploited, until they are finally worn away by the acid of the market. (Lohman, 1993, pp. 157–158, 161)

The two main life preservers that the rescuers offer the world are education and economy, otherwise known as print and price, alphabet and money, bank books and school books. All "developed" peoples must be able to *spell* and *spend*. However, what the rescuers view as tools of salvation, the rest of the world experiences as the things that cast them further adrift. As Dove (1996) insightfully argued, what the rescuers flaunt as "additions" to societies, recipients experience as "subtractions":

> Development interventions are typically conceived as some type of "addition," which is based on the premise that underdevelopment is caused by some type of "absence." . . . The problem with this approach is that it shifts attention away from the international community's own role as resource degrader and focuses instead only on its potential role as "helper." I suggest that the international community needs to ask not just what it can do to help, but also what it must do to stop

hurting. The cessation of most deforestation depends not on stimulating benevolent intervention by the international community, but on halting existing predatory interventions and not initiating any new ones. (Dove, 1996, pp. 60–61)

This is the root confusion befuddling Euro-American "revolutionaries": What they view as tools of rescue, much of the rest of the world experiences as tools of dissolution—not life preservers, but life eroders. We the Euro-Americans—and I include Paulo Freire here—spend a lot of time and money trying to help the rest of the world learn our economic system or learn our educational system, alpha-numeric competency being a prerequisite for successfully monetized minds.

We believe that we are compassionate. We do not like to see suffering. The Buddha said: "Cease to do evil, learn to do good, that is the way of the awakened ones." Well, it seems as if our habit is to rush into the "doing good" part without doing the "ceasing" part. I think that is because the ceasing part does not involve going out to three quarters of the world and being the "good guys." The "ceasing" part means staying home in the well-off quarter and going to the fancy addresses in Rosedale (Toronto), or Westmount (Montreal)—or their equivalent swanky neighborhoods in Chicago, New York, Boston, Seattle, Los Angeles—and addressing the men-in-suits behind iron fences who make the decisions that lead to bombs being dropped, forests being razed, rivers drained, or peoples being monetized and "literatized" thousands of miles away.

MONEY: LIFEBLOOD OF THE DISEMBEDDED ECONOMY

In 1944, Polanyi wrote what amounts to an "instruction manual" for our weird new civilization—kind of a *Euro-America for Dummies*, you might say—and he titled it *The Great Transformation*. Polanyi identified four "fictions" of this new civilization: (a) the illusion that pieces of the earth's surface could be owned by individual members of one species ("land ownership"); (b) the fiction that leasing humans was noble, whereas slavery—owning humans—was immoral ("labor"); (c) the fiction that colored paper and metal could abstractly represent almost everything of value ("money"); and (d) a superstitious faith in "hugely fictitious bodies" ("corporations"; Polanyi, 1957, pp. 68, 71, 130, 178–179). These four fictions dissolved a society's roots; they dissolved the essential connections between people and people and between people and place.[2] The economy, which used to be something nested and controlled within the society, began to switch places with it and set the rules governing society. Stanfield (1986) summed up Polyani's insight in the following way: "Unnatural exchange, aimed at money making pure and simple rather than reproducing a community and sustaining amicable relations, is the root of Polanyi's concept of the disembedded economy" (p. 10).

In 17th-century England, the "disembedded economy" makes its abrupt and fateful appearance, eventually spreading across Europe and fueling the most astonishing explosion of human migration in the earth's history. Between the years 1821 and 1932 alone, 34 million people immigrated to the United States from Europe, while 16 million went to Canada, Argentina, and Brazil. It is important to note that in some years almost half of these immigrants were "re-immigrants"; that is, they were doing wage-labor in America for the second or third time, having returned home to an "enclosed" Europe desperate to buy a *pied a terre* in their true "indigenous" homelands. A shortage of ownable land at home led Europeans to claim lands abroad—a kind of real-life game of musical chairs, albeit one with a more tragic outcome. Thus the "enclosure" of southern Africa, Australia, New Zealand, and America can only be understood against the earlier enclosure of England and Europe. The desperate scarcity of the means of life created by the ravages of enclosure and the other three fictions of capitalism (leaseable humans, currency, rise of corporations) created "homeless" masses eager to invade and claim the "new world" (Rasmussen, 2001, p. 9). The ecological implications of European migration patterns are equally disturbing. As Nabhan (1998) points out, when a map of species extinction is superimposed

---

[2] Op. cit., pages 68, 71, 130, 178–179.

on a map of European migration patterns, the areas of greatest migration are also the areas of the highest level of plant and animal extinctions (p. 45).

Today, the almost unquestioned ideology of price means that from left to right, the entire political spectrum labors under the assumption that to be nonmonetized is to be "poor" or "undeveloped." Price congeals value; everything is measured in terms of currency or capital—social capital, intellectual capital, natural capital, human capital. Euro-American civilization tends to be synonymous with monogenerational and monolingual consumer households, themselves synonymous with acceleration. Each year, the industrial world burns up a million years' worth of stored fossil fuels.

Now, the Rescuers might say: We're only trying to help; we want to put a safety net in place. But isn't a safety net something you provide to people who are going to do something dangerous? Why do Euro-Americans do this dangerous thing? Why are we encouraging others to do it? What is it? What makes our lives dangerous?

Euro-American civilization is nonsocial. We have lost the building blocks of society before we even start—food, shelter, clothing, medicine have all been locked up, made scarce, enclosed; the only way to unlock the requisites is to have the key: money, colored paper. But can you sense the built-in surrender here? Do you hear it every day at work, too? In order to get this colored paper, you are going to have to sell your lifetime in increments to others. This means choosing between life hours shared with your family/community/land (un-waged) or leasing your life hours to a fictitious body (corporate or government) for money. And because the latter option seems like our only choice, "essentially the neighbourhood has gone to work" (Hochschild, 1997, pp. 26–29).

The Ruling Elite says to the people: The land that used to root you we have taken; the human arrangements that used to connect you we have broken; the pattern-languaged face-to-face myths and stories that once flowed between you and your place we have frozen (in print). Now we will train you to master alpha-numeric symbols in order to make money (from us) in order to get access to the land (we took from you) in order to buy the essentials of life. Economic atheism is not permitted.

Once a people has acquiesced to the ideologies of print and price, once they have traded their spirit for spelling and spending, then it is not much of a stretch to get folks to reach out for rescue. One of the major theorists of "rescue" was Paulo Freire. Let us now imagine what Nunavummiut might say if Freire arrived in the North today to teach them his "liberatory pedagogy."

PAULO FREIRE AS "RESCUER"

Men are not built in silence, but in word, in work, in action–reflection. (Paulo Freire)[3]

Freire called for "intervention," "liberation," and "transformation"; he called for the "oppressed" to rescue themselves with the help of his liberatory pedagogy. Freire's admonishment of the nonliteratized for their "semi-intransitive," "submerged" (Freire, 1973, p. 3), and animal-like consciousness clearly places him in the cultural evolution school of thought, which holds that civilizations evolve up a ladder of development from nonmonetary and nonliterary to the apex of the monetized and print-knowledge-dependent. Educators have long believed that conferring literacy on members of an oral culture would make them, in Havelock's words, "wake up from the dream" (quoted in Stuckey, 1991, p. 78). In Freire's words, they abandon "magical explanations" and "hopelessness"—"they emerge"—"no longer mere spectators, they uncross their arms, renounce expectancy, and demand intervention" (Freire, 1973, pp. 17, 13). Havelock and the Freireans argue that, "Nonliterates must be brought into fuller life,"[4] and that only by "reading the word" can you "read the world" (Freire & Macedo, 1987). Stuckey (1991) calls this the "superiority-from-literacy" argument. In this view, literacy not only "makes minds," it "makes minds intelligent" (Stuckey, p. 78). The rescuers' doctrine says that "primitives" evolve as children do, "by acquiring the sort of

---

[3] Freire, P. (1970). *Pedagogy of the oppressed.* New York: Seabury Press.
[4] Stuckey, E. (1991). *The violence of literacy* (pp. 80–83). Portsmouth, NH: Heinemann Educational Books.

intellect we expect of a good reader," most notably a vigorous sense of individuality, the capacity to think logically and sequentially, the capacity to distance oneself from symbols, the capacity to manipulate high orders of abstraction, and the capacity to defer gratification (Postman, 1982, p. 46).

Individualized, competitive, argument-oriented literacy, what Gouldner calls the Culture of Critical Discourse (CCD), tends to cosmopolitanize and uproot civilizations; it breaks their multigenerational links and molds the atomized remnants into mobile human rental units:

> The culture of critical discourse . . . devalues tacit, context-limited meanings . . . while it authorizes itself . . . as the standard of all "serious" speech . . . CCD experiences itself as distant from (and superior to) ordinary languages and conventional cultures . . . it is conducive to a *cosmopolitanism* that distances persons from local cultures, so that they feel alienation from all particularistic, history-bound places and from ordinary, everyday life. . . . (Gouldner, 1979, pp. 26–29, 59)

In Canada's north, European attempts to transform the Inuit way of life have been almost uniformly disastrous. Relocating Inuit to zones lacking in animal life in order to assert Canadian sovereignty resulted in starvation and social disintegration. Next the rescuers introduced "welfare colonialism," creating dependencies, shattering links of sharing practices, stealing children in order to give them a "proper" education. A proper education meant that not only was Inuktitut not permitted, neither was silence. For in Euro-American education, blank pages and silence are signs of social dysfunction: time to call in the counselors and break down the silence, convert it into confession or journal entries:

> Quiet native children were always being told to "speak up," and encouraged to compete with each other. Native habits like the silent facial yes and no of the Inuit were stopped in class. . . . The children often felt ashamed because they could not hunt, clean skins or make things, travel, and stand the cold as their old folks could. On the other hand they considered the older people rather ignorant and old-fashioned. The old closeness between all ages had been broken. (Crowe, 1974, p. 198)

For a pedagogy rooted in alphabetized communication, blank pages typically say nothing to the reader; silence is similarly disdained. And yet for civilizations steeped in the oral tradition and fluent in "pattern languages" like music, quiescence is just as important as activity. The oral tradition may be "high context," but to Europeans it is "low status" (Bowers, 1997, pp. 11–13).

However, Freire's pedagogy negates the space of silence and declares it "inauthentic." Freire asserts that "human existence cannot be silent," and that "knowledge emerges only through the restless, impatient, continuing, hopeful inquiry men pursue in the world . . . apart from inquiry . . . men cannot be truly human" (Freire, 1970, pp. 76, 45–46). This is completely at odds with the Inuit, who believe that "when the teacher is the land, patience and wisdom go together. . . . Things can usually be figured out in time, as long as one is a careful observer." Furthermore, they caution that "there are limits to how much can be achieved in a classroom. . . . [W]isdom can only be gained by engaging with life, by honouring one's heritage and by mastering the skills necessary for independence. We used to have this when we lived on the land" (Nunavik Educational Task Force, 1992, pp. 12, 55).

This honoring of wisdom and heritage seems to contradict Freire's statement that people focused on "their sphere of biological necessity" focus "almost totally (on) survival and lack a sense of life on a more historic plane" (Freire, 1973, p. 17). They "confuse their perceptions of the objects and challenges of the environment," says Freire, but here perhaps it was he who was confused, if we compare the accounts provided by anthropologist George Wenzel, who spent several years with the Inuit in Nunavut, Nunavik (Northern Quebec), and Greenland. Wenzel says that producing "*niqituinnaq*," or "foods that are 'real,' country foods"

> requires specific and essential cognitive ordering by Inuit with regard to animals and by animals to men. If an animal is to choose to participate in the food process, the Inuk harvester must approach the animal with an attitude of respect, and he must intend that the products of the animal's generosity will be available to all." (Wenzel, 1991, p. 139)

Betraying an obsessive human specialness, Freire warns that the nonliterate may be "so close to the natural world that they feel more part of this world than the transformers of the world," resulting in "almost a state of non-being," unable to become "more fully human" (Freire, 1973, pp. 105, 145). However, Nunavummiut do not experience this closeness to the natural world as less than human or merely human, but as more-than-human:

> Ortega y Gasset's statement, "I am I and the environment," synthesizes the kind of meaning Inuit impart when they speak about *niqituinnaq*—a unity of environment, community and human identity . . . harvesting is not just the means by which food is extracted from the natural environment, but also the critical medium through which the human and animal communities are joined together. . . . The fundamental . . . (belief) is that a reciprocity exists between hunter and animal, between one person and another, and between the human community and the natural environment." (Wenzel, 191, pp. 137, 141)

The individual thinker, surveying, naming, and arguing with his world, could be called Freire's orthodoxy. But in "Inuit heritage, learning and living were the same thing," and "knowledge, judgment and skill could never be separated. In institutional life these things are frequently pulled apart and never reassembled. For example, schools spend much of their energy teaching and testing knowledge, yet knowledge by itself does not lead to wisdom, independence, or power" (Nanuvik Educational Task Force, 1992, p. 15). Freire was evidently trying to get across the message here that a comrade should "think for oneself"; however, this obscures the complex authorship of ideas and what Gee (1988) calls the "social nature of interpretation":

> Types of texts and the various ways of reading them do not flow full blown from the individual soul (or biology); they are the social and historical inventions of various groups of people. . . . One doesn't think for oneself; rather, one always thinks for (really *with* and *through*) a group—the group which socialized one into the practice of thinking. And of course, one "thinks for" different groups in different

contexts . . . (since) the literacy practices of these groups are always fully embedded in their whole repertoires of social practices, going well beyond language and literacy per se. . . . (pp. 209–210)

Freire strove to give the individual peasant and worker control over the means of knowledge-production, as he saw it. Freire's liberatory pedagogy in essence focused on knowledge as a print-based product, and it aimed to give the individual worker or peasant the ability to interpret and control this product for him or herself. Freire had no quarrel with the Euro-American civilization that spread the ideology of literacy, the civilization that spread the notion of language as nonsilent, the notion of knowledge as print-based product, the notion of education as the means of knowledge-production. Freire constructed his pedagogy as a life preserver for the oppressed, but he treated oppression as a *fait accompli*; he never seemed to take aim at the "poisons" that dissolve rooted societies in the first place.

FIRST, CEASE TO DO EVIL. . . .

Twenty years ago my partner and I were involved in the East Timor issue in Canada. Indonesia, supported by the United States, Canada, Britain, and Australia, had occupied the tiny Portuguese colony of East Timor in one of the most brutal military occupations of the past century. We called our group the East Timor Anti-Intervention Committee, and, by reading business journals, we had figured out that bullets from a factory in Quebec were making their way into Indonesian rifles and putting holes in Timorese people. In addition to bullets, Canada was shipping tanks and helicopter engines to the military, and, with mining interests factored in, our country was the biggest Western investor in Indonesia. When we approached several church and human rights groups about doing something, they always asked the same two questions: When were you in Timor? How do you propose to get aid in there?

Well, we were never in East Timor, and we were not proposing to *send* anything there. On the contrary, what we wanted to try to do was stop things from being sent there—things like bullets, tanks, helicopter engines. But it's amazing how quickly one is discredited if one hasn't been to a place: How can you know anything? How can you presume to help?

"Solidarity" was the favored approach back then. "We're in solidarity with Nicaragua," folks would say, and they would pile onto a plane and head down there to build a hospital or a school.

Clare Culhane, Canadian peace activist and prison abolitionist, put it best when she used to talk about fighting within the "belly of the beast." In a personal interview that took place in 1985 she told me:

> You know, I was in Vietnam during the war. I worked in a hospital, but it was turned into a military base. . . . I had to make one of the toughest decisions of my life—to stay or go. . . . I went to the Vietnamese embassy in France and I told a guy there my story. He said, "The bombs are falling on our heads, and they will keep on falling even if you're here. Why don't you go home and stop the bombs from coming here."

"Cease to do evil, learn to do good." . . . Obviously things must be done in this order; there is no point in offering a drink of water to someone whose neck is under your boot. What Clare was saying is exactly the same as Snyder's advice on how to save the environment: "Stay Put" (Snyder, 1995). Stop with the thieving and killing already. As long as our way of life is causing most of the problems that the rest of the world has to deal with, the best thing we can do is deal with our own way of life. Stay put, and take everything the *Economic Journal* said in 1960 and reverse it: Do not generate dissatisfaction, unhappiness, social and cultural upheaval, suffering, and dislocation. As long as we need 80% of the rest of the world's stuff, we are going to end up having to go next door and bully people to get it. Rushing around the world thinking we're being neighborly, proselytizing our alpha-numeric fetishism, and narrowing down rich physical-oral-mental cultures into lonely consumers and dazed human "leasees" only burdens the planet with more people like us. And while Euro-Americans traipse around abroad, our economic system at home finds ever new ways to rob, destroy, and pollute faraway lands. Meanwhile we pat ourselves on the back because we, "the rescuers," are out in the igloo or under the banyan tree teaching liberatory pedagogy to the suffering natives so that they can fight back and resist. But wait a sec—if we had cleaned up our backyard, maybe they wouldn't need our salvation, and maybe our pedagogy is not helping them maintain or regenerate their cultures anyway. Let us not presume to do good until we have ceased to do evil. This ought to be the essence of a pedagogy for the oppressor—first, cease to do evil. Next, study our own behavior. In his book, *The White Arctic*, sociologist Robert Paine (1977) said that his one "message" to Whites was to drop the illusion that they were "in the Arctic to teach the Inuit," and instead focus on "learning about white behaviour" (p. xii).

Nunavut, for example, doesn't need to be rescued; and as my Inuit colleagues say exasperatedly, Nunavut definitely doesn't need any more "experts." Mothers in Nunavut have twice the allowable levels of dioxins in their breast milk. In the small community of Qikiqtarjuaq (population: 499), just east of where I live, over 60% of the Inuit children under the age of 15 and almost 40% of Inuit women of childbearing age were found to have PCB body burdens exceeding "tolerable" guidelines.[5] Commoner's recent (2000) "source-to-receptor" research tracked 70% of these dioxins to specific operations in the United States. Nunavut doesn't need Americans to visit; Nunavut doesn't need Americans to come to its rescue; Nunavut needs Americans to "Stay home." Stay home in Ames, Iowa, and Harrisburg, Pennsylvania. These are the communities whose municipal incinerators are producing the dioxins destined for the bodies of the Inuit women of Qikiqtarjuaq. American communities and ours are tied together by America's invisible exhalation of death. America breathes out, and Inuit die. This is what a "pedagogy of the oppressor" needs to teach. Stay home. Go on a field trip to Alpena, Michigan, or Hartford, Illinois. Figure out how to clean it up, slow it down, stop it. It's the Euro-American way of life that needs to be put under the microscope, not intriguing tribes in far-away lands. Instead of exotic slide shows on the Arctic, how about American schools take exotic

---

[5] Government of Canada (1999, November). *A Second Diagnostic on the Health of First Nations and Inuit People in Canada*. Ottawa: Human Resources Development Canada (HRDC).

field trips to Bethlehem Steel's and US Steel's iron sintering plants in Chesterton and Gary, Indiana?—two of the dozen or so key sources of dioxin being exhaled to the Arctic. The dioxin particles rise with warm air and moisture and fall with cold temperatures, "grasshoppering" their way toward the north pole, where it is too cold for them to evaporate and instead they settle, absorbed into lichen, eaten by caribou, and in turn consumed by Inuit. In Coral Harbour (pop. 822), in the middle of Hudson Bay, over half of the annual dioxin burden for 1997 was deposited in just 2 months: September and October—dioxins from Ash Grove's cement kiln in Louisville, Nebraska, from Lafarge's cement kiln in Alpena, Michigan, from Chemetco's copper smelter in Hartford Illinois, from the city of Harrisburg's incinerator in Pennsylvania.

So: You don't have to come to Nunavut. . . . Take my word for it, it's a still a very beautiful place. If you like, I can send you a postcard. In return, maybe you could send me a postcard of the new scrubbers being put into the smokestack in Harrisburg, Pennsylvania. That would be right neighborly.

ACKNOWLEDGMENTS

A special thanks is owed to Jimi Onalik, Sheila Watt-Cloutiec, and Zebedee Nungak for the ideas in this chapter, and to Clare Culhane for her example.

REFERENCES

Barss, P. (2000, August 1). Relative merits: Can cultures impede development? *National Post*, A-15.

Blackburn, J. (2000). Understanding Paulo Freire: Reflections on the origins, concepts, and possible pitfalls of his educational approach. *Community Development Journal* (pp. 6–17). London: Cambridge University Press.

Bowers, C. A. (1997). *The culture of denial: Why the environmental movement needs a strategy for reforming universities and public schools*. Albany, NY: State University of New York Press.

Churchill, W. (1951). *The second world war* (Vol. 5). London: Houghton Mifflin.

Commoner, B., Bartlett, P. W., Eisl, H., & Couchot, K. (Center for the Biology of Natural Systems, Queens College, CUNY). (2000, September). Long-range air transport of dioxin from North American sources to ecologically vulnerable receptors in Nunavut, Arctic Canada. Montreal, Canada: Secretariat of the North American Commission for Environmental Cooperation. Retrieved October 3, 2000, from http://www.cec.org

Crowe, K. (1974). A history of the original peoples of northern Canada. Montreal: McGill Queens University Press.

Cuautemoc, G. (1998, Winter). The real foreign debt: A letter from an Indian chief to all European governments to repay the gold and silver borrowed between 1503 and 1660. Adbusters, 20, 30–38.

Dove, M. R. (1996). Center, periphery, and biodiversity. In S. B. Brush & D. Stabinsky (Eds.), Valuing local knowledge: Indigenous people and intellectual property rights (pp. 58–71). Washington, DC: Island Press.

Freire, P. (1970). Pedagogy of the oppressed. New York: Seabury Press.

Freire, P. (1973). Education for critical consciousness. New York: Continuum.

Freire, P., & Macedo, D. (1987). Literacy: Reading the word and the world. South Hadley, MA: Bergin & Garvey.

Gee, J. P. (1988). The legacies of literacy: From Plato to Freire through Harvey Graff. Harvard Educational Review, 58 (2), 206–221.

Gouldner, A. (1979). The future of intellectuals and the rise of the new class. New York: Seabury Press.

Griffin, S. (1995). The eros of everyday life. New York: Doubleday.

Hochschild, A. (1997, May/June). Home work time: Why are we working more and spending less time at home? Mother Jones, 26–29.

Kloppenburg, T. (1991). No hunting! Biodiversity, indigenous rights, and scientific poaching." Cultural Survival Quarterly, 15 (3), 10–18.

Lohman, L. (1993). Resisting green globalism. In W. Sachs (Ed.), Global ecology: A new arena of political conflict (pp. 157–167). London: Zed Books.

Nabhan, G. (1998). Cultures of habitat: On nature, culture, and story. Washington, DC: Counterpoint.

Nunavik Educational Task Force. (1992). Lachine, Quebec: Makivik Corporation.

Paine, R. (Ed.). (1977). The white arctic: Anthropological essays on tutelage and ethnicity. St John's, Newfoundland: Memorial University of Newfoundland Press.

Polanyi, K. (1957). The great transformation. Boston: Beacon Press.

Postman, N. (1982). The disappearance of childhood. New York: Delacorte Press.

Rasmussen, D. (2001). The seven not-so-wonders of the world and other challenges of modern Europeanness. Forests, Trees and People newsletter (No. 43), 7–11. Uppsala, Sweden: Swedish University of Agricultural Sciences.

Snyder, G. (1995). A place in space: Ethics, æsthetics, and watersheds. Washington, DC: Counterpoint.

Stanfield, J. R. (1986). The economic thought of Karl Polanyi. New York: St. Martin's Press.

Stuckey, E. (1991). *The violence of literacy*. Portsmouth, NH: Heinemann Educational Books.
Wackernagel, M., & Rees, W. (1995). *Our ecological footprint: Reducing the human Iimpact on the earth*. Gabriola Island, BC: New Society Publishers.
Wenzel, G. (1991). *Animal rights, human rights: Ecology, economy and ideology in the Canadian arctic*. Toronto: Toronto University Press.

8

How the Ideas of Paulo Freire Contribute to the Cultural Roots of the Ecological Crisis

C. A. Bowers

One of the challenges in assessing the merits of Paulo Freire's eman-cipatory pedagogy is that his ideas are so widely promoted in leading colleges of education that criticism of his ideas will, in effect, be a criticism of these institutions. The challenge is further magnified by subtle changes in his thinking during his last years that suggest his concern with how he was being interpreted by his followers. In *Mentoring the Mentor: A Critical Dialogue with Paulo Freire* (1997), he titled a subsection of the chapter he wrote in response to his followers "Allowing Me Also to Continue Growing and Changing in My Con-texts." Indeed, his philosophical anthropology, which he articulates so forcefully in *Pedagogy of the Oppressed* and in *Education for Critical Consciousness*, would appear at first glance to be fundamentally at odds with the Freire found in *Mentoring the Mentor*. Witness the es-sentialist assumption about human nature that he universalizes in

133

Pedagogy of the Oppressed (1974) when he states that to "exist humanly, is to name the world, to change it. Once named, the world in its turn reappears to the namers as a problem and requires of them a new naming" (p. 76). Near the end of his life he writes:

> What I have been proposing is a profound respect for the cultural identity of students—a cultural identity that implies respect for the language of the other, the color of the other, the gender of the other, the sexual orientation of the other, the intellectual capacity of the other; that implies the ability to stimulate the creativity of the other. But these things take place in a social and historical context and not in pure air. These things take place in history, and I, Paulo Freire, am not the owner of history. (1997, pp. 307–308)

To state the challenge of assessing the ideas of Freire more directly: Should he be viewed as an essentialist thinker whose philosophical anthropology is based on Western assumptions that were also the basis of the Industrial Revolution, or should he be understood primarily as an advocate of dialogue and a cultural sensitivity that precludes imposing on other cultures a Western understanding of the emancipated individual? I think the answer can be found in how his philosophical anthropology continually reasserts itself even as he writes in *Mentoring the Mentor* about the need to avoid a paternalistic relation to the oppressed and the need to understand that the meaning of democracy has to take account of specific historical and cultural contexts (pp. 307, 308). For example, his philosophical anthropology underlies his warning that if teachers over-romanticize the students' language, they "are not engaging with their students in a mutual process of liberation" (p. 307). His philosophical anthropology also frames his understanding of the teacher as a mentor. As he puts it:

> The fundamental task of the teacher is a liberatory task. It is not to encourage the mentor's goals and aspirations and dreams to be reproduced in the mentees, the students, but to give rise to the possibility that the students become the owners of their own history. This is how I understand the need that teachers have to transcend their merely instructive task and assume the ethical posture of a mentor who truly believes in the *total autonomy, freedom, and development* of those he or she mentors. (p. 324; italics added)

Here he restates his belief that the essence of being human is the ability to continually create anew the conditions of one's own existence. This view of "total autonomy" is summed up in his statement that "to speak a true word is to transform the world" (1974, p. 75).

It is important to note that neither Freire nor his followers questioned whether consistency with their own position would require that members of different cultures be allowed to express their own views on whether total autonomy is the core feature of a fully realized human being. Apparently, the members of different cultures that have not been liberated, and thus cannot speak a true word, need not be consulted on such an important question as what constitutes humankinds' essential nature. Neither McLaren nor Giroux, who are two of the leading proponents of Freire's ideas, have been troubled by Freire's abstract pronouncements on a universal human nature that ignores the profound differences in cultural epistemologies. McLaren (1995), for example, claims that "We (teachers) need to occupy locations between our political unconsciousness and everyday praxis but at the same time be guided by a *universal emancipatory worldview* in the form of a provisional utopia or contingent foundationalism" (p. 59, italics added). While I must admit to not understanding what McLaren means by a "provisional utopia" or a "contingent foundationalism," it is abundantly clear that his use of the phrase "universal emancipatory worldview" is a restatement of the Freirean assumption that each generation should rename the world, and that their achievements should be overturned by the generation that follows them. Ironically, even though McLaren is correct in his assessment of the dangers of economic globalization, he does not recognize that the ideal of universal emancipation is based on the same assumptions and silences that underlie the language of globalization. Giroux's understanding of the mission of a critical pedagogy is also based on the Freirean assumption that to be fully human is to engage in a continual world-transforming process. In *The Pedagogy and Politics of Hope* (1997), he writes:

> Critical pedagogy would represent itself as the active construction rather than the transmission of particular ways of life. More specifically, as transformative intellectuals, teachers would engage in the invention of language so as to provide spaces for themselves and their

students to rethink their experiences in terms that both name the
relations of oppression and offer ways to overcome them. (p. 224)

I think a strong argument can be made that the promotion of Freirean
ideas in leading graduate schools of education, as well as the recent
efforts to restore the ideas of John Dewey to a prominent place in
the curriculum, can be traced to the deep cultural assumptions these
thinkers share with other elite groups that are continually mislabeled
as conservative capitalists. In effect, I suggest that the uncritical
embrace of Freirean emancipatory ideals and pedagogical practices is
largely accountable in terms of a sociology of knowledge insight into
how people tend not to recognize as problematic, and thus criticize,
what they take for granted. Or in Bateson's (1972) terms, thought occurs when there is "a difference which makes a difference" (p. 318).

What has not been widely recognized by Freire or his followers
is that there are no real differences between the deep cultural assumptions that underlie his philosophical anthropology and his more
recent emphasis on dialogue, and the Western cultural assumptions
that underlie the current digital stage of the Industrial Revolution—
which universities promote in the language of the marketplace one
might expect to find in corporate boardrooms. The shared assumptions can be seen by comparing the Freirean ideal of individuals who
are totally free from the oppressive traditions of their communities—
what he calls the "alienating daily routine that repeats itself" (1985,
p. 199)—with the form of individualism required by the Industrial
Revolution. In writing about the early 19th century Luddites' resistance to the destruction of their communities, Sale (1995) sums up
the form of individualism required by the new industrial model of
production and consumption in the following way:

All that "community" implies—self-sufficiency, mutual aid, morality
in the marketplace, stubborn tradition, regulation by custom, organic
knowledge instead of mechanistic science—had to be steadily and
systematically disrupted and displaced. All of the practices that kept
the individual from becoming a consumer had to be done away with
so that the cogs and wheels of an unfettered machine called "the
economy" could operate without interference, influenced merely by
invisible hands and inevitable balances. (p. 38)

If we refer to various statements about the purpose of a liberal education, we find that emancipating individuals from "all that 'community' implies" has been a longstanding goal, one that is not unique to
Freirean thinkers.

Freire's ideas were formed initially in response to Third World
situations where a history of colonialism had created great economic
disparities and silenced all forms of resistance. That his philosophical anthropology, and the cultural assumptions that underlie it, now
support the new forms of colonialism being resisted by many Third
World cultures can be seen in Berthoud's recent (1992) observation
of what is being undermined by the Western model of economic
globalization. Especially noteworthy is that the first sentence in the
following quotation, which is Berthoud's summary of what is required
by the Western model of economic development, could have been
taken from any number of Freire's writings—as well as the writings
of his followers:

> What must be universalized through development is a cultural com-
> plex centered around the notion that human life, if it is to be fully
> lived, cannot be constrained by limits of any kind. To produce such
> a result in traditional societies, for whom the supposedly primordial
> principle of boundless expansion in the technological and economic
> domains is generally alien, presupposes overcoming symbolic and
> moral "obstacles," that is, ridding these societies of various inhibiting
> ideas and practices such as myths, ceremonies, rituals, mutual aid,
> networks of solidarity, and the like. (p. 72)

In effect, what the Western approach to development needs to overturn are the same "symbolic and moral obstacles" that Freire and his
followers view as sources of oppression.

The irony of how the Freirean approach to emancipation, even
when it starts with decoding local cultural patterns, contributes to
the current process of globalization becomes easier to recognize when
we consider specific cultures that are attempting to regenerate their
traditional symbolic foundations as sources of self-reliance, as well as
sources of resistance to the latest wave of colonization that derives
its legitimacy from the reductionism of Western science and technology rather than from the other-worldly orientation of the church.

These cultures of resistance—the Andean peasants working to recover their ancient system of agriculture; the Balinese who rejected
the Green Revolution by returning to their temple ceremonies for
regulating the allocation of water and the planting of rice crops; the
grassroots efforts of the Zapotista to retain their traditional patterns
of community rather than be subjugated by the modern political and
economic systems of a centralized government; the indigenous farm-
ers in India who rebelled against the industrial model of agriculture
that was being carried to a new level of exploitation by Monsanto's
genetically engineered "terminator" seed—all utilize their own
culturally based approaches to critical reflection as a necessary part
of their resistance. But they do not rely on it as the only legitimate
source of knowledge and authority. Rather, their mythopoetic narratives are the basis of their ceremonies, systems of moral reciprocity
and mutual aid, patterns of intergenerational mentoring, use of technology, and ways of understanding human/nature relationships. By
making critical reflection the only legitimate approach to knowledge,
and by framing this process in a way where each generation is to
overturn what has survived from emancipatory efforts of the previous generation, the Freirean approach to emancipation undermines
the deep symbolic foundations on which these and other indigenous
cultures are based.

   This process of undermining the symbolic basis of resistance to
the Western cult of progress and autonomous individualism is hard
to recognize because of the "God-words" invoked by Freire and his
followers to legitimize their mission. Words and phrases such as
*emancipation, freedom, dialogue, liberation, transformation rather than
transmission, critical inquiry rather than a banking model of education,*
are difficult to question without appearing as a reactionary thinker.
These "God-words" are further immunized from serious questioning
by the fact that some traditional cultures carry on practices that do
not fit widely held standards of social justice, such as the "honor"
killings practiced in some Middle East cultures, the continuation of
caste systems that still lock people into horrific forms of existence,
and the practices of gender discrimination—to cite a few examples.
And there are many situations where previous processes of colonization make the limited use of the language of emancipation a valid

approach to empowerment—limited in the sense that specific traditions of oppression are the focus of emancipation. This qualification
brings out an important distinction, namely, that Freire's language
of emancipation is based on the Western assumptions that underlie
his philosophic anthropology, which leads to viewing all traditions as
oppressive in nature.

The double bind inherent in the thinking of Freire and his followers is that although an emancipatory pedagogy may raise awareness
in ways that enable people to recognize changes that need to be
made, it cannot be the basis of community—which requires multiple
forms of knowledge and relationships that are not always dependent
on the critical reflection and the perspective of the individual. Freire
may have viewed himself as changing in ways not fully grasped by
his followers, but I think that he retained to the end a core set of
assumptions or metacognative schemata (that I have described elsewhere as root metaphors; 1995, 1997, 2000, 2001). These include the
following: a human-centered view of human/nature relationships,
thinking of change as linear and inherently progressive in nature,
representing critical inquiry and thus the autonomous individual as
the only legitimate source of agency and moral authority, and most
important of all, assuming that the view of reality based on these assumptions should replace the "realities" constituted by other cultural
epistemologies. It is important to reiterate the connection between
these assumptions and the form of consciousness required by the
Industrial Revolution—and, by extension, the cultural mediating
characteristics of computers. These assumptions included thinking
that change is constant and the surest sign of progress, that individuals should be emancipated from cultural traditions and networks of
mutual support, that this is a human-centered world, and that differences in cultural ways of knowing need to be replaced by a universal
mindset that makes individual self-determination the highest form of
existence.

There are several other important connections between the cultural assumptions that are the basis of Freire's thinking and the assumptions on which the Industrial Revolution was based. And just as
these assumptions continue to undermine cultural diversity and self-
sufficient communities in the name of globalization, they continue

to be reproduced in the thinking of Freire's followers. The effect is that their proposals for educational reform, if put into practice, would further undermine community by emphasizing that only new ideas that have survived the process of critical inquiry should be the basis of daily life. In effect, they would be experimental ideas in that they have not been tested in the life of the community. The view of progress that Freire and his followers share in common with today's proponents of economic and technological globalization involves the rejection of what makes communities more than a collection of critically reflective individuals who, in lacking what can only be learned within communities, are dependent on consumerism.

Although using different legitimating metaphors, both Freire and the proponents of the Industrial Revolution were against all traditions. The irony is that the quest to overturn traditions in order to create dependency on new technologies and to expand markets, as well as the Freirean formula of equating all traditions with oppression and thus impediments to living full, self-determining lives, are expressions of a Western tradition that Shils (1981) calls an "antitradition tradition" (pp. 235–239). Freire's (1974) claim, for example, that "to speak a true word is to transform the world" (p. 75) is itself part of the Western philosophical tradition that holds that rational thought does not have to be held accountable for the diversity of cultural patterns or the importance of these patterns in people's lives.

Traditions are as complex and varied as the world's cultures. If the next generation of educational reformers are going to understand why a more complex understanding of the nature of tradition is important to noncolonizing approaches to multicultural education, as well as recognize the alternatives to the consumer-oriented culture that is trashing the environment, professors in graduate schools of education will need to expand the list of required reading to include Shils' book, *Tradition* (1981). This book does not represent what many formulaic thinkers, in encountering the word *tradition*, will conclude is another expression of reactionary thinking. Rather, it is a description of the many cultural patterns and practices that are repeated over four generations of cohorts, and an explanation of why these everyday patterns and practices should be called traditions. It is also a book that clarifies how traditions should be understood, including how some traditions were wrongly constituted in the first place, how some traditions change too slowly whereas others disappear before we fully understand their importance in our lives, how they change from without and from within, and the many misconceptions that surround the nature of tradition, including the two extremes. One extreme and incorrect view of tradition is that it does not change; the other view, which is equally incorrect, is that people can live better lives if they are free of all traditions. The importance of Shils' book is that it provides us with a more complex way of understanding the continuities in cultural experience without essentializing them. It also provides a basis for understanding the differences between cultural groups such as the Taliban, which has an extremely reactionary approach to tradition, and other cultures that are recovering the attenuated traditions necessary for resisting Western pressures to adopt a modern, progressive form of consciousness. The adequacy of a Freirean understanding of multiple dimensions of tradition, especially how traditions can be the basis for resisting colonization, can be more fully considered by students if the following are added to the required reading list:

- *Grassroots Post-Modernism: Remaking the Soil of Cultures* (1998), by Gustavo Esteva and Madhu Suri Prakash;
- *The Spirit of Regeneration: Andean Culture Confronting Western Notions of Development* (1998), edited by Frédérique Apffel-Marglin with PRATEC;
- *Global Ecology: A New Arena of Political Conflict* (1993), edited by Wolfgang Sachs.

The nature of wisdom refined over generations of collective experience, to cite another aspect of tradition that cannot easily be reconciled with Freire's Enlightenment assumptions, can be found in such books as Ross' *Returning to the Teaching: Exploring Aboriginal Justice* (1996) and Basso's *Wisdom Sits in Places: Landscape and Language Among the Western Apache* (1996).

Another assumption that Freire and his followers share with the proponents of the consumer-and-technology-dependent lifestyle now being globalized by the modern heirs of William Cartwright and

Henry Ford is that human progress can be understood without consideration of its impact on the environment. Indeed, the collective silence in the writing of Freire and his followers about the environmental crisis is really quite astonishing. Freire does not mention it at all, and the only reference I have seen by critical pedagogy theorists is McLaren's inclusion of the word "environment" in a list of current problems. That Freire and his followers have not acknowledged what has become such a dominant concern of people around the world that even CEOs of major corporations are beginning to rethink their priorities can be accounted for by the way in which their language creates a double bind. The source of the double bind, and thus their silence, is in the way their basic assumptions underlie the industrial form of culture that is a major contributor to the ecological crisis. The consequence is that, just as tradition has to be treated in a formulaic manner in order to preserve the conceptual consistency of the Freirean language of emancipation, the language that most accurately describes the essential challenge of the environmental movement also has to be dealt with in formulaic fashion.

Environmentalists concerned with reversing the present decline in the viability of natural systems speak of the need to *preserve* species, to *conserve* wilderness, and to *restore* habitat. These metaphors cannot be reconciled with the language of liberalism and the cult of progress. Nor can the metaphors that describe the characteristics of ecologically sustainable cultures, and that enable us to address ecojustice issues, be reconciled with assumptions underlying the worldview of liberalism and the Freirean view of emancipation, as I explain later. The recovery of the environment and community are essentially conserving activities, which are not to be identified with how Freire and his followers think of conservatism. They ignore the many forms of conservatism—including temperamental conservatism, cultural conservatism (which takes as many forms as there are languages), and philosophical conservatism—by equating conservatism with capitalism and globalization. This aspect of their formulaic thinking reproduces the popular mistake of confusing conservatism with what is, in fact, Classical Liberalism, which is based on assumptions they share. To restate the double bind inherent in Freirean thinking, if they were to recognize the cultural roots of the ecological crisis, they would have to engage in a process of reconceptualization that could only be carried through by their ceasing to be Freirean theorists. And too many reputations would be threatened for them to acknowledge that their emancipatory pedagogy is based on earlier metaphorical constructions that did not take account of the fact that the fate of humans is dependent on the viability of natural systems.

The social justice issues of class, race, and gender that are now the focus of attention of Freire's followers, and that received increasing attention during Freire's last years, should not be treated as separate from the cultural changes that will be required if we are to limit our adverse impact on the environment in ways that allow ecosystems to recover. Defining social justice in terms of gaining equal participation in the consumer-and-technology-dependent lifestyle represents a preecological way of thinking. Reforming public schools and universities in ways that contribute to ecojustice should now be the main focus of attention, and the issues of class, race, and gender should be understood within the context of this more inclusive challenge. In providing an overview of the different dimensions of ecojustice, and the curricular reforms necessary to achieving it, I extend at the same time my critique of the core assumptions Freire, even in his later years, took for granted.

Defining ecojustice in ways that take account of the environmental impact of our increasingly technological and consumer-driven culture, as well as differences in cultures resisting this juggernaut, is a daunting task. As a starting point, four aspects of ecojustice stand out as having particular importance for how we think of educational reform. These include: (a) ecoracism, which involves minority and marginalized cultural groups who are exposed to toxic chemicals in their workplace and neighborhoods; (b) the need to reduce the hyperconsumerism of the middle class while raising the material standard of living for the millions of children and adults in Third World countries who experience poverty in their daily lives; (c) conserving the traditions of noncommodified knowledge, skills, and relationships within minority cultures, as well as regenerating the more attenuated noncommodified traditions within the middle class; and (d) ensuring that the lives of unborn generations will not be diminished by a degraded environment.

Addressing these issues will require developing a critical under-standing of the connections between the high-status knowledge acquired in our educational institutions and the relentless drive to create new technologies and markets. This will involve understand-ing how the metaphorical nature of language frames current ways of thinking in terms of earlier expressions of cultural intelligence that equated change with progress, that represented humans as able to control and now reengineer the genetic basis of life, and that uni-versalized the ideal of the autonomous individual. It will also involve a critical understanding of the Janus face of science, particularly science's role in the expansion of the Industrial Revolution as well as how its current usefulness is being compromised by its increasing integration into corporate culture.

Curriculum reforms should also take account of the myth, cur-rently given new life by the promoters of computers, that represents abstract knowledge, such as that found in print, as more reliable and culturally advanced than oral forms of encoding and communicating. This myth, along with its supporting assumptions, has resulted in viewing cultures that are more ecologically centered as too primitive to learn from. Overlooked in the current rush to replace as much of face-to-face communication and accountability as possible with computer-mediated communication is that this technology repro-duces the mind-set and thus the form of subjectivity described in the quotation taken from Sale's book. Computers can only process explicit and decontextualized forms of knowledge. In addition, they reinforce the myth that language is a conduit through which people pass their ideas and objective information, and they reinforce a sub-jective experience of temporality where the past and future become a matter of subjective judgment and perspective. The realities—the contextual and tacit nature of most of our cultural knowledge, the metaphorical nature of language that encodes and carries forward earlier culturally specific ways of knowing, and the traditions we are dependent on and that can easily disappear, such as what has hap-pened to our traditional sense of privacy rights—are being further undermined in ways that have important ecojustice implications. While Moravec (1988) announces that computers represent the transition to the "postbiological phase of evolution" (p. 4) and Turkle

(1995) sees in Internet experiences the possibility of thinking of ourselves as "fluid, emergent, decentralized, multiplicitous, flexible, and ever in process" (pp. 263–264), the reality is that computers are a colonizing technology that undermines intergenerational knowledge that is the basis of cultural diversity. It is important to note that while Freire and his followers have been deeply critical of capitalism, they have ignored the role of computers in creating a world monoculture based on the more environmentally destructive characteristics of the Western mind-set. Some of his followers have even suggested that computers can be part of the emancipatory process.

A whole paper could be written on curriculum reforms that address the causes and effects of ecoracism. Although not meaning to diminish the importance of ecoracism, I want to turn to another area of curriculum reform that highlights a fundamental weakness in the Freirean/critical pedagogy way of thinking. That is, I want to focus the discussion of curriculum reform on the forms of knowledge that critical inquiry may help us understand as important, including why they have been marginalized, but that are based on profoundly different relationships and forms of authority. These reforms relate directly to the need to reverse the cultural patterns that contribute to the community and environmentally destructive cycle of increasing dependence on consumerism that leads to the need to work longer hours, often at two jobs, and that reduces the amount of time for parenting and community involvement, while returning more waste and toxic materials to the environment, including the neighborhoods of politically and economically marginalized groups. The amount of waste produced by the American middle class is staggering. According to Hawkin, Lovins, and Lovins (1999), "industry moves, mines, extracts, shovels, burns, pumps, and disposes of 4 million pounds of material in order to provide one average middle-class family's needs for a year" (p. 51). The changes resulting from the more than 80,000 synthetic chemicals introduced into the environment in recent years that support this lifestyle, as well as the rapid rate of global warming that has resulted in 40% of the polar ice cap melting away, are equally staggering.

It is in what universities have relegated to the category of low-status knowledge, and in what the emancipatory educational theorists have labeled variously as the *transmission* and *banking* models of education, that we find the forms of knowledge and relationships that represent alternatives to a consumer-dependent lifestyle. These forms of knowledge and relationships also contribute to the vitality of community, that is, the whole range of interactions and skills that have not been commodified. These include the myths (or what I prefer to call the mythopoetic narratives), ceremonies, rituals, patterns of mutual aid, and networks of solidarity that Berthoud (1992) refers to as sources of resistance to the cult of progress and the form of self-centered individualism this cult requires.

Low-status knowledge also includes the communal craft and agricultural knowledge that William Morris, a leading 19th-century British socialist, viewed as the alternative to the dehumanizing effects of liberal/industrial thinking. Personal skills and talents expressed in communal activities ranging from growing, preparing, and sharing food—which Esteva and Prakash (1998) say are at the "heart of community and communion" (p. 53)—to musical performances, healing, and repairing the material forms of culture that have become worn but are still useful, are all dependent on the sharing of intergenerational knowledge. In such areas as gardening, woodworking, and playing or making an instrument, we can see how this knowledge is carried forward through mentoring relationships that involve more than the transferring of information. Mentoring also involves passing on wisdom about relationships, the importance of doing something well by mastering what has been done before—and adding to it through one's personal talent and insight—all aspects of character development that have an important influence on the formation of self-identity and moral reciprocity within the community.

In summarizing the essential characteristics of low-status knowledge, I want to acknowledge that in some communities these patterns may be based on rigid, even reactionary thinking and that long-held prejudices and special interests may be sources of social injustice. Having acknowledged what I take to be an already widely held understanding that I feel compelled to restate in order not to be seen as romanticizing low-status knowledge, I want to summarize its essential characteristics, which will be expressed in culturally diverse ways. Low-status knowledge and relationships are primarily dependent on face-to-face communication, and thus are contextually grounded and involve interpersonal accountability that we do not find in print-based communication. Low-status knowledge and relationships also involve intergenerational accountability that is fundamentally different from high-status knowledge, which is abstract and theory-based, experimental, and nonaccountable in terms of communities—and non-Western cultures. Low-status knowledge is largely passed on as the fund of tacit knowledge that has been tested and refined over generations. In addition, it often it encodes the intergenerational experience of living in one place over many generations. Most importantly, in being noncommodified it has a smaller ecological footprint than the high-status knowledge that enables the individual to participate in the culture of hyperconsumerism.

Educational reforms that address ecojustice issues ranging from contaminated environments, undermining traditions of moral reciprocity and self-reliance, and jeopardizing the prospects of future generations, will need to combine a critical and comparative cultural understanding of the historical roots and current manifestations of high-status knowledge with the more difficult task of helping students recognize and participate in the noncommodified aspects of community life. Suggesting that the curriculum should introduce students to the many expressions of noncommodified knowledge and relationships within their neighborhoods, as well as the noncommodified traditions carried forward by other cultural groups still intergenerationally connected to traditions that have survived the pressures of assimilation, is a daunting challenge. It is not that these forms of knowledge and relationships are difficult to understand in the same way that abstract theories are difficult to grasp. Rather, the difficulty lies in not being able to recognize the patterns we take for granted—and that our high-status education creates a prejudice against taking seriously. How many of us can identify the noncommodified relationships, activities, skills, and knowledge that are part of our daily routines? Or to ask the reverse question, how many of us can give an account of the daily patterns that have been commodified? And do we understand the environmentally and communally destructive consequences of the products and expert systems that we depend on?

A starting point, which can begin in the early grades and be carried on through graduate school in ways that bring the historical and cultural epistemology issues into the foreground, is to do a survey of the noncommodified activities and relationships within the students' neighborhood. This survey can then be extended to a consideration of the noncommodified traditions still carried on by groups who identify themselves with a distinct cultural legacy that is the basis of their experience of community. An ecojustice-oriented curriculum also needs to connect students with the networks of mutual aid, and to help them develop personal talents that contribute to community and that can serve as the basis of their taking on the responsibility of mentoring the next generation.

After students obtain an understanding of the range of noncommodified aspects of daily life, which will be fewer in mainstream culture and more widespread and varied in minority ethnic groups who have been economically marginalized, students then need to consider the short and long term consequences of extending the commodification process into more areas of daily life. This will involve learning how different cultural forces contribute to this process. For instance, as students progress through the educational process, they need to consider the cultural mediating characteristics of technology—the way in which technologies undermine important traditions and create new forms of dependency, contribute to the loss of personal skills, and influence patterns of thinking—and the political processes that will bring the introduction of new technologies and expert systems more under democratic control. Similar questions need to be asked about the increasing role that scientists play in undermining traditions of self-sufficiency within communities and in contributing to a global monoculture of consumers. These are the forms of learning and participation upon which multicultural education should be centered. It could just as easily be called *environmental education* in the broadest sense of the phrase. However, ecojustice is the preferred phrase because it highlights the interconnections between viable, interdependent ecosystems and viable, interdependent communities—and that our future depends on maintaining the widest possible diversity in cultural approaches to sustainable living.

In summary, I want to emphasize what I see as the conceptual biases that prevent Freire and his followers from addressing ecojustice issues. These include:

- His emphasis on viewing humans as possessing a universal essence ignores how this represents an Enlightenment way of thinking that does not take account of cultural differences in ways of knowing and subjectivity.
- His view of the nature of change ignores the different ways in which cultures interpret the past and its relationship to the present and future.
- By recognizing critical reflection as the *only* genuine source of knowledge, which is one of the chief characteristics of a print-based form of consciousness, Freire delegitimates other forms of knowledge and intergenerational communication that are often the basis of mutually supportive communities.
- The anthropocentric nature of his pedagogy, while largely unnoticed by Western thinkers, further undermines cultures that have developed complex systems of interspecies communication and moral reciprocity with the natural world.

Until graduate programs in education are revised in ways that recognize that Freire's assumptions are shared by proponents of globalization, and that these assumptions undermine local knowledge that is the basis of resisting this colonizing process, the rhetoric of emancipation will continue to contribute to the double binds that make our future increasingly problematic.

REFERENCES

Apffel-Marglin, F. (Ed. with PRATEC). (1998). *The spirit of regeneration: Andean culture confronting western notions of development*. London: Zed Books.

Basso, K. (1996). *Wisdom sits in places: Landscape and language among the Western Apache*. Albuquerque, NM: University of New Mexico Press.

Bateson, G. (1972). *Steps to an ecology of mind*. New York: Ballantine Books.

Berthoud, G. (1992). Market. In W. Sachs (Ed.), *The development dictionary: A guide to knowledge as power* (pp. 170–187). London: Zed Books.

Bowers, C. A. (1995). *Educating for an ecologically sustainable culture: Rethinking moral education, creativity, intelligence, and other modern orthodoxies.* Albany, NY: State University of New York Press.

Bowers, C. A. (1997). *The culture of denial: Why the environmental movement needs a strategy for reforming universities and public schools.* Albany, NY: State University of New York Press.

Bowers, C. A. (2000). *Let them eat data: How computers affect education, cultural diversity, and the prospects of ecological sustainability.* Athens, GA: University of Georgia Press.

Bowers, C. A. (2001). *Educating for eco-justice and community.* Athens, GA: University of Georgia Press.

Esteva, G., & Prakash, M. S. (1998). *Grassroots post-modernism: Remaking the soil of cultures.* London: Zed Books.

Freire, P. (1974). *Pedagogy of the oppressed.* New York: Seabury Press.

Freire, P. (1985). *The politics of education: Culture, power, and liberation.* South Hadley, MA: Bergin & Garvey.

Freire, P. (Ed.). (1997). *Mentoring the mentor: A critical dialogue with Paulo Freire.* New York: Peter Lang.

Giroux, H. (1997). *Pedagogy and the politics of hope: Theory, culture, and schooling.* Boulder, CO: Westview Press.

Hawken, P., Lovins, A., & Lovins, L. H. (1999). *Natural capitalism: Creating the next industrial revolution.* Boston: Little, Brown.

McLaren, P. (1995). White terror and oppositional agency: Toward a critical multiculturalism. In C. Sleeter & P. McLaren (Eds.), *Mutlicultural education: Critical pedagogy and the politics of difference* (pp. 117–144). Albany, NY: State University of New York Press.

Moravec, H. (1988). *Mind children: The future of robot and human intelligence.* Cambridge, MA: Harvard University Press.

Ross, R. (1996). *Returning to the teachings: Exploring aboriginal justice.* Toronto: Penguin Books Canada.

Sachs, W. (Ed.). (1993). *Global ecology: A new arena of political conflict.* London: Zed Books.

Sale, K. (1995). *Rebels against the future: The Luddites and their war on the industrial revolution.* Reading, MA: Addison-Wesley.

Shils, E. (1981). *Tradition.* Chicago: University of Chicago Press.

Turkle, S. (1995). *Life on the screen: Identity in the age of the internet.* New York: Simon & Schuster.

Afterword

C. A. Bowers

A new set of priorities is needed for assessing current graduate programs of education that will influence future generations of teacher educators—including teacher educators from other countries who obtain their advanced degrees from Western universities. Regardless of whether these graduate programs are based on the ideas of Freire, Dewey, Whitehead, Vygotsky, Gardner, constructivist theorists, or more technicist approaches to educational reform, they must be held to the new standards of accountability now dictated by the irrefutable evidence that human demands are exceeding the regenerative capacity of natural systems. Current efforts to globalize the hyperconsumer, technology-dependent lifestyle taken for granted in Western societies will further accelerate the destruction of the environment. It is unlikely, however, that the Western media dream machines and corporate policies will do anything more than raise expectations that cannot be fulfilled except for small segments of the population in Third World countries. For the majority of Third World people, the future is more likely to be low-wage employment in factories that are not required to meet adequate environmental standards, living in the midst of toxic waste, and the loss of the intergenerational knowledge that reduces the need for consumerism. Even with globalization still in its early stage of development, the Western consumer lifestyle has had a destructive impact on the environment that threatens the prospects of future generations. The human prospects have been further undermined by the sheer increase in the world's population, which is now over 6 billion people, and has adversely impacted the environment—even in remote areas that have not been influenced by modern expectations.

The degree and rate of environmental changes, which most Westerners encounter in the form of print or electronic media reporting that competes with sporting events and various forms of television entertainment, have immediate and long-term implications that few people fully comprehend. Not even the scientists documenting the changes in the world's oceans and climate can predict with any real degree of accuracy who will be most affected. They are even less capable of predicting the cultural changes that will be dictated by environmental forces that exceed our ability to control. However, people living in different bioregions are beginning to learn that their further impoverishment and toxic-related illnesses cannot be reconciled with the Western myth of progress. The decline in the world's fisheries has impacted communities in nearly every part of the world, and the increasing scarcity of potable water signals further degradation in the quality of everyday life—and further raises the likelihood of armed conflict. The worldwide loss of topsoil is now estimated at 36%, with the remaining soil being increasingly degraded by the need to use chemicals to increase productivity. Global warming, which is now predicted to leave major cities and even some countries vulnerable to rising ocean levels, is contributing to more extreme weather patterns and to radical changes in the habitats that plants, animals, and cultures have adapted to. With the melting of glaciers and polar ice, not even the North Atlantic Current, which carries the warm water that maintains Europe at between 9° and 18° Fahrenheit warmer than would otherwise be the case, can be taken for granted. The introduction in the last 50 years or so of hundreds of thousands of synthetic chemicals into the earth's ecosystems has also set in motion changes in reproductive patterns among different species and in the ability of our bodies to ward off illnesses. That the average North American now has some 84 chemicals ranging from PCBs to dioxins in their bodies brings the element of an uncertain future, including early death, to everybody. The list of the many ways the environment is being degraded could be endlessly extended.

Although our shopping malls, expanding suburbs, and media are still able to create a sense of abundance of life necessities and even luxuries, the reality is that the average Western lifestyle is not based on the kind of ecological intelligence that our future survival depends on. We are still relying on the form of cultural intelligence that was based on assumptions about unlimited progress in our ability to control (and now redesign) nature, to continually grow the economy, and to equate consumerism and a life of conveniences with happiness. The challenge will be to find, within our own mix of Western cultural traditions, the basis for a form of ecological intelligence that enables us to live more community-centered and less environmentally destructive lives—as many cultures around the world already have achieved through centuries of respecting the limits of their environments. Indeed, there are groups in North America and in other Western regions that place the emphasis on supportive relationships within the community and on environmental stewardship rather on keeping up with the latest consumer fads and getting ahead as individuals. Developing ecological intelligence, which has taken many cultural forms of expression, is not only achievable for us—it is an absolute necessity. But it will be difficult for reasons expressed by the contributors to this book, namely, that the same mind-set that created the problems we are now experiencing cannot be used to solve them. In terms of colleges and departments of education, the mind-set that continues to emphasize that the teacher's role is to foster a greater sense of individual creativity and expression, to promote economic growth by reinforcing students to think and communicate in ways that are mediated through technologies, and to see the answer to social justice issues as a matter of assimilating marginalized ethnic minorities into a middle-class consumer lifestyle, will further exacerbate the problem. These educational goals will not lead to changing the deep cultural assumptions that underlie our ecologically destructive form of intelligence.

Unfortunately, this mind set is not limited to colleges of education. As I point out in *The Culture of Denial* (1997), universities are largely responsible for the distinction between high- and low-status knowledge. High-status knowledge is the basis of the seemingly endless stream of new technologies, a higher material standard of living for certain segments of the population, the ability to access abstract knowledge and thus to live a lifestyle less dependent on intergenerationally tested experiences and responsibilities, and the myth that the ever-expanding monetization of knowledge, skills, and relationships is the basis of happiness and progress. The conceptual double bind that the promoters of high-status knowledge are caught in prevents them from recognizing how it impedes the development of an ecological form of intelligence. As high-status knowledge (and lifestyle) continues to be based on the deep cultural assumptions about the autonomous nature of the individual, the linear nature of progress, anthropocentrism, and a view of the rational process that is supposedly free of cultural influence, it is unable to recognize that it is a major contributor to the increased rate of environmental degradation we are now experiencing. Ironically, the environmental focus of many professors has not really addressed the cultural roots of the ecological crisis, with the result that environmentally oriented courses are little more than add-ons and exercises in ecomanagement. This criticism is not meant to dismiss the efforts of these professors. Rather, it is meant to highlight that these well-intended efforts are caught in a double bind that ensures the continuation of cultural practices that will eventually overwhelm the ability of ecomanagement approaches to come up with stop-gap solutions.

High-status knowledge not only leads to a lifestyle that has an unsustainable ecological footprint, it is also responsible for marginalizing and even undermining the forms of knowledge, relationships, and skills that are more ecologically sustainable. What universities have relegated to low status, and thus not worthy of learning, includes the knowledge and relationships that sustain the intergenerational life of culturally diverse communities. These excluded forms of knowledge and relationships are learned and renewed in individualized ways through face-to-face relationships that often take the form of mentoring. Contrary to the modern prejudice, what has been relegated to low status encompasses the organic complexity of orally based cultures. These cultures involve a greater emphasis on shared assumptions about mutual aid and moral reciprocity than the increasingly commoditized character of high-status knowledge. Among these different cultures and subcultures, moral relations within the community and between humans and the environment may be rooted in mythopoetic narratives, rather than in the reductionist and secularizing sciences that make values more a matter of subjective judgment and the pursuit of self-interest where the only sense of being part of a larger whole is the Darwinian world of survival of the fittest. The knowledge and relationships that sustain these communities, many of which were described by the contributors to this book, have been relegated to low status and thus not part of the discourse considered legitimate within high-status circles. As a result, the contribution these cultures could make to the development of ecological intelligence is being ignored by our educational institutions. One of the unfortunate consequences of high-status knowledge is that students from Third World cultures often reproduce its biases when they return to their home cultures.

Indoctrination into the patterns of high-status knowledge has another limitation that has not been mentioned. As the various academic disciplines are based on deep cultural assumptions formed in the distant past, the ways of thinking and material expressions of culture they help constitute and sustain never adequately account for how our daily lives are embedded in today's complex network of relationships. The shopping mall that represents the highest achievement of rational design, synthetic materials that represent the latest scientific and technological advances, psychological studies of how to stimulate the need to consume, and so forth, often leave people feeling that important aspects of their lives are being ignored or stifled. This frequently takes the form of feeling pressured to conform to the expectations of experts who design the mesmerizing technologies and social spaces. This same lack of symmetry often exists between the requirements of the work or educational setting and the need for meaningful relationships and a sense that life has a purpose beyond that of working in order to avoid being overwhelmed by consumer debt. The house that contains the latest conveniences and the three-car garage, and that is placed in a setting that limits conversations with neighbors, relatives, and involvement in other nonmonetized community activities, may also be experienced as limiting. The point is that many of the needs of personal fulfillment and meaningful relationships are met in everyday experiences that make up the complex ecology of face-to-face, intergenerational relationships that universities have relegated to low status. These ecologies of face-to-face relationships may be the object of academic research, but the university is not the place where students learn about who the mentors are in the community and the many different nonmonetized activities that lead to the development of personal interests and talents. Nor will students learn about other aspects of their communities, such as who the storytellers are and who can help connect them to embodied experiences of place. In effect, the embodied aspects of daily experience, where personal identity and meaning are fulfilled or left undeveloped by the particular pattern of relationships, may provide alternative ways of developing ecological intelligence. Indeed, I argue that the largely ignored aspects of the intergenerational life of communities, even in their attenuated state, represent part of the answer to reducing our impact on the earth's ecosystems while at the same time meeting psychological and spiritual needs we are wrongly attempting to fulfill through consumerism.

But there is another aspect of the double bind that must be addressed before we consider how the aspects of individual/community life can help us recognize the direction that the reform of colleges of education should take in order to be ecologically accountable. Colleges and departments of education share with the more prestigious academic disciplines a core set of assumptions, with two of them being that institutionally (and now online) based education is the engine of modern progress and that this form of learning will emancipate individuals, here and in other parts of the world, from the deadening hold of tradition. Education professors are more inclined to emphasize the creative and idea-generating capacity of the student's own experience, whereas in other parts of the university the emphasis is more on the power of expert knowledge as the source of progressive ideas, technologies, and lifestyle changes.

   As pointed out in the earlier analyses, Freire gives change ontological status and views it as linear and progressive in nature. The
followers of Freire and Dewey, the proponents of child-centered education (who are in the tradition of Rousseau, Freud, Carl Rogers, and
Piaget and his more recent interpreters), the advocates of adapting
education more closely to the needs of competing successfully in a
global economy, and the advocates of technology-mediated learning, all view education as fostering change. And their view of change
is generalized to encompass all of the world's cultures. They share
with other segments of the university the deeply held bias that traditions are the enemy of progress, even though their individual lives
involve the reenactment and individualizing of a complex network of
traditions. That is, they share an institutionally learned interpretive
framework that does not take account of the cultural patterns they
reenact on a daily basis. Conceptually, they are conditioned to be
aware of the plethora of changes that result from the integration of
high-status knowledge, technological inventiveness spurred on by
corporations, and a media industry whose profits depend on packag-
ing these changes as the latest expression of progress and the good
life. This emphasis on change has resulted in not asking the question
marginalized by the Industrial Revolution, and now by the progressive orientation of the high-status knowledge industry: What do we
need to conserve for the sake of sustaining more morally coherent
and less ecologically destructive communities ("communities" being
used here as interchangeable with cultures)?
   This orientation toward change, and the assumption that it is
always progressive in nature, does not correspond to our individual
experience—or even the experience of the ideologues and experts
who are today's apostles of change. Nevertheless, it is at the center of
the double bind that prevents us from addressing the ecological crisis
in ways that do not rely on the earlier form of cultural intelligence
that gave conceptual direction and moral legitimacy to the Industrial Revolution. The emotional response, as well as the formulaic
thinking triggered among most promoters of high-status knowledge
(both in schools and in universities) when the words "conserve" and
"tradition" are used, is really quite astonishing, particularly when
these same people claim also to be the arbitrators of what constitutes

social justice in a multicultural world. The use of the word "conservatism" is even more likely to elicit a hostile response, except for social groups who mistakenly think of themselves as conservatives when, in reality, their economic and other assumptions should be more correctly identified as Classical Liberalism. This source of confusion about political metaphors can also be laid at the doorstep of political science departments for failing to provide students an historical perspective on the origins and changes that characterize the different expressions of liberalism and conservatism. And in not understanding the different expressions of conservatism—temperamental, cultural, economic, religious, philosophical, and what I call cultural/bioconservatism—the public discourse about multicultural and environmental issues continues to be conflicted in ways that undermine considering, as the basis of reform, the proven alternatives to community and environmentally destructive lifestyles. Referring to environmentalists as liberals (a habit of groups who believe in minimizing the role of government and in the "invisible hand" that ensures that competition brings out of the best in people and technology), and referring to corporations and the politicians they are able to buy as conservative, are both examples of the confused state of our thinking.

In suggesting that colleges and departments of education in particular, and other university departments more generally, should be focused on conserving ecologically sustainable cultures and local community practices, I am likely to be attacked as dangerous and irresponsible, and to be totally dismissed. Thus, there is a need here to explain more fully why a conservative rather than a liberal orientation is the way out of the double bind of globalizing a consumer lifestyle based on Western liberal assumptions. To reiterate why the use of a Freirean pedagogy in non-Western cultures failed, the following must be kept in mind: (a) local resistance to being assimilated to Western patterns of thinking; (b) local emphasis on conserving intergenerational patterns of mutual aid, moral reciprocity, and the craft skills that such Western thinkers as William Morris viewed as the alternative to the industrial process that brutalized the British landscape and people; and (c) local traditions of ecologically sensitive technologies that have been developed over generations of experience within a bioregion. These expressions of conserving in environments where there is little room for error avoid the contradictions in current thinking about multicultural education where the emphasis is on assimilation into a modern, progress-oriented culture. As activists working within indigenous cultures that are attempting to renew their traditions of self-sufficiency will point out, decolonizing approaches to education place the emphasis on conserving and renewing intergenerational knowledge, and not on giving students the abstract knowledge that leads them to leave their villages in search of the modern dream of making it on their own—which usually means a life of extreme poverty in urban shanty towns.

Educating teachers to indoctrinate their students with the idea that the changes they envision will always have a progressive effect, which too often results in a career in the corporate world or in some other institution that orchestrates change in accordance with the assumptions underlying expert knowledge, is clearly wrong. If we are going to take multiculturalism and the ecological crisis seriously, teachers need to be educated in ways that help students understand which intergenerational traditions need to be conserved, radically revised, or abandoned entirely. This involves a more complex understanding of when critical thought is appropriate: that is, knowing the destructive nature of prejudging *all* traditions as being inherently outmoded. As a member of a Peruvian non-governmental organization dedicated to helping the indigenous cultures of the Andes preserve their traditions of nurturing biodiversity, Ishizawa points out that the ability to conserve the intergenerational knowledge that supports self-reliance and patterns of mutual support is dependent on the ability to listen—to listen to the stories and experiences of the members of the community. It also involves the ability to understand the antitradition traditions of science, technology, and Enlightenment ideals in a way that combines both critical analysis and an ability to acknowledge positive contributions to improving the quality of life and to mitigating the modern impact on the environment. In short, the only way out of the double bind is to shift the emphasis from educating teachers in the Freirean and Deweyian methods that promote taken-for-granted attitudes toward change to an emphasis on helping students recognize what needs to be conserved, and how conserving—in the many forms it may take, depending on the culture—contributes to an ecologically sustainable future. Freire was correct in associating critical reflection with empowerment. His mistake was in arguing that each generation has to overturn the knowledge of previous generations. Increasingly, as Western technologies become more widespread, critical reflection enables communities and cultures to preserve what remains of their traditions of self-sufficiency by clarifying the forms of subjugation that often accompany new technologies that have, for example, produced genetically modified seeds, enabled computer-mediated distance education, and industrialized eating habits and entertainment.

One of the most important contributions of the chapters in this book is the way in which their authors highlight the difference between Freire's understanding of intelligence as centered in the individual's capacity to initiate change through critical reflection and the ecological intelligence of many indigenous cultures. Freire, like other Western thinkers, continues the tradition of representing the individual as separate from the world that is to be acted on. In effect, the individual is viewed as the primary social unit. This requires treating the traditions of community (in both the Western and the indigenous worlds) as a constraint on individual self-determination, and critical reflection as the only source of emancipation and legitimate knowledge. Thus, this approach to knowledge contributes to progress by substituting the judgment of youth for the knowledge of the community that has been tested and revised over generations. Classical Liberals, as well as today's mislabeled "conservatives," rely on this same assumption that the individual is the primary social unit. Both emphasize how individuals realize their highest potential through competition and material gain. Constructivist educators also share Freire's view of the individual, but emphasize the need to nourish the individual's inner and more subjectively based resources— that the constructivists assume will lead to a better society. These modern extrapolations on the Western view of individualism serve as examples of how deep cultural assumptions, which I have described elsewhere as root metaphors or metacognitive schemata (Bowers, 1995, 1997, 2001), prevent us from recognizing how daily experience is embedded in a cultural ecology of interactive and interdependent relationships—and from recognizing how these assumptions underlie cultural practices that are undermining the environment.

The metaphor *ecology* has been taken over by the sciences, which may lead many readers to think that my reference to a cultural ecology is an inappropriate use of the term. However, if we go back to the original meaning of the ancient Greek word "oikos," before Ernst Haeckel in 1866 transformed it into "œcologie" and used it to represent the study of the natural environment, it referred to the operations and management of the family household. By recovering the ancient Greek meaning of the word, it is possible to avoid the limitations of viewing intelligence as an attribute of the autonomous individual. The metaphor of "household" can be extended to the larger patterns of interaction and interdependence that we find in community, culture, and the way in which cultures are embedded in natural systems.

Gregory Bateson's more contemporary way of understanding ecology helps us recognize that the Cartesian world of supposedly separate organisms, objects, and autonomous individuals does not take account of the interactive nature of life-forming and sustaining processes. For Bateson, the key to understanding existence, whether at the molecular or cultural level, are the patterns that connect—and how these interactions involve information exchanges that influence both the internal development and external behavior of all of the life forms that make up an ecological system. The "household" for Bateson encompasses systems within larger systems: from the cell with its microecology of DNA, RNA, proteins, and enzymes to humans whose conceptual maps influence which human and environmental interactions will be recognized and how they will be responded to.

Unlike the Western (and Freirean) tradition of locating intelligence in the observing, reflecting individual, Bateson understood the most basic aspect of intelligence (which he refers to as a unit of information or idea) as emerging from what he calls "a difference which makes a difference." That is, the patterns that connect with other patterns are the source of information that circulates through the ecological system as a whole. As he put it in *Steps to an Ecology of Mind* (Bateson, 1972), "A 'bit' of information is definable as a difference which makes a difference. Such difference, as it travels and undergoes transformation in a circuit, is an elementary idea" (p. 315). He goes on to represent the interactive and connected nature of intelligence in the following statement:

> The total self-corrective unit which processes information, or as I say, "thinks" and "acts" and "decides," is *a system* whose boundaries do not at all coincide with the boundaries either of the body or of what is popularly called the "self" or "consciousness"; and it is important to notice that there are *multiple* differences between the thinking system and the "self" as popularly conceived. (p. 319)

A difference that make a difference—the change in the facial expression of the person we are talking with, the oncoming sport utility vehicle (SUV) that prompts thoughts of self-indulgence and waste, the emergence of the sun that brings the information exchange between all living entities to a peak level, the decrease in snow pack that precipitates a different exchange of information among all the life forms dependent on it—led Bateson to locate intelligence in interactive patterns that make up a system as a whole. This is profoundly different from locating intelligence in the observing individual. Snyder (1990) gives a more poetic expression to Bateson's insight when he writes:

> The world is watching: one cannot walk through a meadow or forest without a ripple of report spreading out from one's passage. The thrush dart back, the jay squalls, a beetle scuttles under the grasses, and the signal is passed along. Every creature knows when a hawk is cruising or a human is strolling. The information passed through the system is intelligence. (p. 19)

In effect, Bateson is explaining how relationships can be understood as information that undergoes transformation through subsequent interactions—and by extension, that humans need to be understood in terms of their relationships and not as separate beings that reflect and act on an external world.

The following statement brings out another Batesonian insight that is also understood by the Inuit, Quechua, and other indigenous cultures that led the contributors to this book to recognize the limitations of Freire's emancipatory vision. That is, "In no system which shows mental characteristics can any part have unilateral control over the whole. In other words, *the mental characteristics of the system are immanent, not in some part, but in the system as a whole*" (1972, p. 316, italics in original). The consequences of not understanding the long-term disruptions resulting from trying to exert unilateral control over a system as a whole can be seen in the dams along the Columbia River in the United States that now threaten salmon with extinction and have degraded other aspects of this network of ecosystems. It can also be seen in the destructive impact of modern farming techniques on the complex ecosystems that made up the northern grassland prairies that, before the arrival of European settlers, covered nearly a third of what indigenous cultures called "Turtle Island" and European settlers called America. The mental characteristics of the latest attempts of "unilateral control over the whole" can be seen in the globalization of Western technologies and consumerism—which are now immanent in the changes occurring in the Earth's carbon cycle and in the chemistry of other life-supporting systems.

Although Bateson emphasizes that intelligence emerges from the ongoing interactions (difference which makes a difference), and that human intelligence is only one aspect of the larger ecology of mind, he also acknowledges that humans process information in ways that are profoundly different from the biological processes of plants and animals. He introduces the distinction between "map and territory," which he borrows from the mathematical philosopher Alfred Korzybski, as a way of explaining how the metaphorical patterns of thinking handed down from the past serve as the map that enables us to recognize certain aspects of the environment, while putting out of focus other aspects. That is, the differences that we become aware of and respond to are largely determined by our conceptual (cultural) maps. Thus, the conceptual maps of the European immigrants led them to view the forests and prairies as sources of economic opportunities, and to ignore that the land was already settled—and that these still-earlier settlers had a more complex and sustainable knowledge of the ecosystems they depended on. Similarly, the conceptual maps of dominant groups—men, Anglo-Americans, heads of corporations, and so forth—influence what aspects of the territory (culture, natural environment, etc.) they will be aware of, how they will respond to it, and what they will ignore. It is Bateson's understanding of how the conceptual maps (metaphorical thinking encoded in the language) passed down from the past continue to influence how we think that has special significance for reforming colleges and departments of education, which play such an important role in the cycle of perpetuating the myth of the individual as an autonomous thinker.

The "difference which makes a difference" that alters behavioral responses, internal chemistry, and ideas is indeed an expression of change. It is important to note, however, that regardless of whether we are talking about chemical changes at the molecular level or on the scale of global warming, the ongoing changes are not examples of the Western idea of progress. Rather, the point here is that change is integral to living systems. At the same time, the process of authopoisis, or self-making of an organism or social system, involves conserving (that is replicating) previous patterns of development—a point that Freire and his followers ignore. Thus the organic processes of self-making that lead to the development of a mature oak tree, salmon, or linguistically endowed person can be understood as the most basic expression of the conserving nature of life-forming processes, even as both external and internal changes lead to minor variations.

In terms of culture, the process of conserving (which always involves minor variations) can also be seen in the languaging processes that influence how we think and behave, what we are aware of and ignore, and how we understand our personal identity. The individualizing of a culturally shared interpretive framework is part of the "difference which makes a difference" that circulates through the larger cultural ecology, and the rate of change it leads to is largely dependent on the nature of the taken-for-granted cultural assumptions. Thus, even cultures based on the assumption of the autonomous individual and the progressive nature of change conserve, but what they conserve is the relentless pursuit of what is new and the expression of self-interest. Other examples of change-oriented theorists actually conserving long-standing traditions can be seen in how Freire's ideas reproduced (conserved) the taken-for-granted interpretive frameworks of patriarchy and anthropocentrism that can be traced back to the Book of Genesis. Although Freire became aware in his later years that his writings were based on this age-old gender bias, he never realized how he was helping to conserve the cultural assumption that humans are superior to and, thus separate from, nature.

If we examine the thinking of such leading scientists as Richard Dawkins, E. O. Wilson, Francis Crick, and Antonio Damasio, we find that their explanations of the most recent scientific discoveries within their fields are based on the root metaphor of mechanism that was also the basis of thinking of Isaac Newton and Johannes Kepler. The way in which culturally specific root metaphors—individualism, mechanism, change, economism, and, now, evolution—frame thinking in such diverse fields as architecture, agriculture, education, and medicine could also be cited as further examples of how languaging processes conserve, with only minor variation, earlier patterns of thinking. To learn Japanese, French, English, or Quechua is to learn the culture's categories for recognizing relationships and the attributes of the participants in the relationships. The languages also encode the moral codes that are to govern how to act in the relationships. In effect, the conserving nature of language is as inescapable as the conserving nature of DNA—yet both are part of complex ecologies where a "difference which makes a difference" may lead to minor or, over time, significant changes. The irony in terms of thinkers such as Freire and his present interpreters is that they are conserving even as they argue against conservatism.

As conservation and change are integral to biological and linguistic processes, it is really quite pointless to make categorical judgments about either of them. But ideologies—that is, the theories we create to explain how we should think and value various genres of conservatism and liberalism—are another matter. As interpretive frameworks based on root metaphors that reproduce earlier cultural expressions of intelligence, ideologies function in the same way Bateson described the map–territory relationship. That is, an ideology provides the interpretative framework for recognizing certain aspects of the relationships and processes that make up the multilayered ecology that humans are part of. It also influences what will not be recognized, or will be interpreted in terms of past prejudices. For example, different genres of liberalism, with their shared assumptions about progress, individualism, and anthropocentrism, ignored how human activity degrades the environment and undermines the systems of mutual aid within different cultures. That the majority of the world's population base their lives on fundamentally different root metaphors was also part of the territory ignored by the conceptual maps of liberals—to stay with Bateson's metaphor. The different genres of conservatism—economic (Classical Liberalism) and philosophic conservatism—also ignored environmental changes resulting from the lifestyle they promoted. On the other hand, there are religious/cosmology-based forms of conservatism (i.e., Amish, Quechua, Zapotec, Inuit, Hopi) that interpret the industrial-based lifestyle as destructive to their idea of a morally coherent community and their responsibility as stewards of the environment.

The accelerating rate at which the environment is being degraded, and the continuing undermining of the intergenerational knowledge that previously held communities together, strongly suggest the need to question current approaches to educational reform. The modern emphasis on justifying education on the basis that it contributes to more competitive economies, more technological innovations, and more material wealth will only accelerate the ecological crisis that is increasingly impacting people's daily lives. And appeals for educational reforms that will supposedly prepare students to become agents of radical and highly experimental changes also seems to be based on ignorance of the fundamental issues we face. The mentality that underlies the promotion of the World Trade Organization, the drive within universities and other research centers to invent new technologies (whether we need them or not), and the generations of people educated to base their thinking and behavior on the assumptions that co-evolved with the Industrial Revolution is not going to disappear overnight. Indeed, it will remain as a dominant and highly disruptive force in the world. One has only to count the percentage of SUVs on North American roads to realize the number of people who see no connection between their behavior and what the environment can sustain. *Growthmania,* the term Herman J. Daly uses to describe the pathology that North Americans and much of Europe have turned into a civic virtue, will continue to be the dominant reality. A further disturbing sign of the state of consciousness of a large segment of the adult population is the widespread acceptance of corporate America's shameless exploitation of younger and younger children by sending the message that if they do not buy a certain product they are losers.

Given the forces promoting growthmania, and the evidence that we are already overshooting the sustaining capacity of many of the Earth's ecosystems, we need to ask a fundamentally different question, one that is based on the recognition that our future survival depends not on accelerating the rate of innovation and change but on conserving the forms of knowledge, skills, and relationships that will enable the members of different cultures to live less environmentally destructive lives. A corollary question is: How do we conserve linguistic diversity as a basis for ensuring biodiversity? These questions have special significance for classroom teachers as they play an important role in reinforcing the values and ways of thinking of the dominant consumer-oriented culture. They have also demonstrated a capacity to support social movements that are attempting to address social justice issues. Their efforts to challenge gender bias in the curriculum and classroom discussions is evidence that they are capable of recognizing when thought patterns and behaviors are based on an ancient root metaphor no longer reconcilable with today's notions of social justice. Although American classroom teachers were not in the forefront of the feminist and civil rights movements, many of them nevertheless demonstrated a capacity to alter the curriculum in ways that supported these movements. Thus, there is hope that classroom teachers in all Western countries might also begin to address the cultural roots of the ecological crisis—which would mean becoming aware of the many ways in which the classroom reinforces the modern myths of the autonomous individual and the progressive nature of change.

Another minor myth that still holds sway among classroom teachers and professors of education is that people learn from their own direct experience. This widely held idea does not take into account how past patterns of thinking are encoded and reproduced in the language–thought connections that are usually taken for granted. Conversations with classroom teachers as well as with professors of education quickly reveal that, in spite of near daily accounts of environmental disasters and disruptions, they continue to emphasize

the values and ideas largely responsible for these problems. The need
today is to find a way to reorient the thinking of these two groups in
the same way that their thinking was altered by the feminist and civil
rights movements. The goal of this reorientation is to change their
thinking in ways that make conserving, rather than the relentless
pursuit of change, the dominant concern. For educators, a subset of
the general question, "What should we conserve in order to ensure
a sustainable future?" includes the following: What aspects of intergenerational knowledge contribute to morally just communities,
and to empowering its members with the skills that enable them
to be less dependent on consumerism? What traditions within the
culturally diverse communities contribute to more cooperation and
sharing, and how can schools help revitalize these traditions? How
can schools help students become knowledgeable about the mentors in the community, and enter into mentoring relationships that
develop the interests and talents of the students? How can schools
pass on the genuine achievements of modern culture while at the
same time helping students to recognize the importance of elder
knowledge? How can students be helped to recognize that critical
reflection makes its greatest contribution when it is used to renew
intergenerational traditions that strengthen moral reciprocity and
connectedness within the community—and that critical reflection
that leads to radical changes should be focused on specific forms
of injustice? When framed in this way, education that focuses on
conserving community and the environment is addressing ecojustice issues. It is also avoiding the ideologically driven appeals for
universal emancipation that, as recent history has shown, destroyed
the basis of community self-sufficiency, resulted in the centraliza-
tion of power by new elites, and led to the colonization of cultures
that do not share the Western assumptions on which the ideal of
emancipation is based. Questions about what should be conserved,
which should always involve consideration of what needs reforming,
are relevant both to modern and traditional cultures. However, the
former face the special challenge of renewing what remains of the
noncommodified aspects of community, whereas traditional cultures
(in the West and in Third World settings) face both subtle and overt
pressure to adopt the consumer-dependent lifestyle of the modern

world—which seduces their youth into rejecting the traditions of their ancestors before they have gained the wisdom to make these critical decisions.

The suggestion that public schools and universities focus on what needs to be conserved in order to live more sustainable lives is intended to bring them in line with the thinking of environmental groups most knowledgeable about the rapid changes occurring in the earth's ecosystems. That environmentalists are today's true conservatives can be seen in how they label themselves and their projects. For example, we find groups who call themselves "conservation biologists," programs that focus on "wilderness preservation," and organizations such as the Nature Conservancy. The following statements by leading environmental thinkers reveal even more clearly that conservation rather than experimentally oriented progress should be our basic concern:

> The basic value of a sustainable society, though, the equivalent of the Golden Rule, is simple: each generation should meet its needs without jeopardizing the prospects of future generations to meet their needs. (Durning, 1991, p. 165)

> A thing is right when it tends to preserve the integrity, stability, and beauty of the biotic community. It is wrong when it tends otherwise. (Leopold, 1949/1966, p. 262)

> Sustainability is embedded in the processes that occur over long periods of time and are not always visually obvious. It follows that ecological design works best with people committed to a particular place and the kinds of local knowledge that grow from that place. This knowledge is slowly accumulated, season by season, through active engagement with the land. (Van Der Ryn & Cowan, 1996, p. 65)

> For local indigenous communities, conserving biodiversity means to conserve the integrity of ecosystems and species, the rights to resources and knowledge, and their production systems based on biodiversity. (Shiva, 1996, p. 1)

The conservative orientation of environmentalists can also be seen in their increasing reliance on the "precautionary principle" as a basis for challenging the introduction of new technologies and changes in government policies that are deemed environmentally destructive. The precautionary principle as formulated in 1998 by a group of scientists, environmentalists, government researchers, and labor representatives from the United States, Canada, and Europe states that: "When an activity raises threats of harm to human health or the environment, precautionary measures should be taken even if some cause-and-effect relationships are not fully established scientifically" (quoted in Rampton & Stauber, 2001, p. 124). This is a statement that Edmund Burke, the founder of philosophical conservatism, could have written.

The shift from the liberal ideology used to justify the World Trade Organization and the North American Free Trade Agreement to a mind-set (ideology) that recognizes that conserving vital living systems is the only way to ensure a sustainable future can be seen in the efforts of Hawkin, Lovins, and Lovins (1999) to document the changes leading to what they refer to as the "next industrial revolution" (p. 9). Although they do not adequately address how to subordinate the profit motive to other values, they make several key points about the shift in consciousness occurring within segments of the business community as well as in city planning. The conservative orientation that some businesses are beginning to adopt is in the recognition that the environment, as "natural capital," should be preserved—even expanded. And the best example of a conserving orientation to city planning can be seen in the Brazilian city of Curitiba. There is much to criticize in their book, *Natural Capitalism* (1999). Nevertheless, it represents an important step in the reconceptualization of the environmentally ruinous ideas and values still held by most corporations. It is also important for documenting how efforts to mimic natural processes in nature are leading to changes in methods of production.

The study of indigenous cultures, the writings of Bateson and other environmentalists who address how cultures are nested in natural systems, and even businesses and governmental agencies that are beginning to recognize the double bind of relying on liberal assumptions as a basis for conserving the viability of the environment provide important insights into the nature of ecological intelligence. Although ecological intelligence may be expressed in many different ways, depending on how the local environment has shaped the traditions of the culture, there seem to be essential characteristics that must be taken into account in thinking about educational reforms, especially the reforms that need to be undertaken in colleges and departments of education. These include: (a) an awareness that the individual is nested in culture, and that the culture is nested in natural systems; (b) an awareness that intelligence is not the attribute of the autonomous individual, but is initially constituted through the process of language acquisition that carries forward earlier patterns of metaphorical thinking and interacts with the patterns of the other nonhuman participants that make up the larger ecology; (c) an awareness of how intergenerational knowledge that knits the community together is conserved through processes of renewal that engage the interests of the younger generation as well as develops their personal talents; (d) an awareness that moral reciprocity must extend beyond the family and community in ways that include natural systems; and (e) an awareness that an ecological interpretation of democracy means, as Bateson (1972) put it, that no group in the larger ecology can have "unilateral control over the whole" (p. 316).

The characteristics of ecological intelligence are not simply a theoretical construct. Rather, they can be seen in the cultural practices of many indigenous cultures that led the contributors to this volume to recognize the Western assumptions that are the basis of Freire's view of critical reflection. Ecological intelligence can also be seen in the practices of ethnic and other social groups in the West: in the communitarian movement, in groups who are attempting to practice voluntary simplicity in their daily lives, in religiously based groups such as the Amish and Mennonite, in the efforts of communities to develop the use of local currencies, and even among academics who are beginning to recognize the moral and conceptual double bind inherent in working within institutions dedicated to globalizing a modern form of consciousness. It is particularly visible in the growing practice of applying the principles of ecological design, such as found in the Bateson Building in Sacramento, California, and in the vernacular approach to buildings found in many regions of the world.

The question is likely to be raised about why the emphasis here is on reforming colleges and departments of education and, in particular, teacher education programs. The answer is quite simple: Schools are one of the few places in society where socialization can be broadened to include comparisons between the student's own culture and the practices of other cultures, where students can obtain an historical perspective on cultural practices that represent hard-won achievements and other practices that were either morally problematic in the first place or environmentally destructive, where students can acquire the language that enables them to develop conceptual maps that more adequately represent the interactive nature of ecosystems and the impact that cultural practices have on them. The successful efforts of corporations in the United States to turn hallways, classrooms, and uniforms into marketing opportunities would seem to make my suggestion appear to be out of touch with the realities of school subcultures. And the lack of attention to how cultural beliefs and practices impact ecosystems in professional education classes, as well as the liberal ideology that frames thinking about pedagogy and curriculum, would seem to be further evidence that schools are not sites where significant reforms can be made. In spite of the increasing visibility of corporate values, a few teachers are beginning to address environmental issues in ways that go beyond teaching students about the importance of rain forests and recycling. That student awareness of the ecological crisis often exceeds that of their teachers is another source of hope. And over the last few years there has been a growing awareness on the part of a small group of professors of education that the environment now represents the most significant challenge we will face in the years ahead. In spite of the impediments to radical reform of colleges of education, and the indoctrination to a modern, consumer-oriented lifestyle that most students are exposed to, we really have no choice about where our reform efforts should be directed.

The urgency of reform can be put in focus by asking how many generations of students will be affected in the course of a teacher's career? Can the environment survive the consumer-dependent lifestyle — the sport utility vehicle (SUV), three-car garages, electronic gadgets, endless fads in eating, clothes, entertainment, etc. — that the current generation of students is being socialized to take for granted? Our technologies may be able to compensate for certain shortages, such as water, electricity, or petroleum products, but the environment and the quality of life of people in the Third World will be even further degraded. The underclasses in our society will also be further victimized by the materialistic interpretation of success being promoted in most public schools and universities.

Even though we have no guarantees that we can achieve the change in consciousness on the scale required to avert the further consequences of global warming and other changes resulting from overshooting the sustaining capacity of the environment, it is nevertheless important to spell out the direction that educational reform should take. I use the word "ecojustice" as a more inclusive way of thinking about educational reform. As used here, it takes account of different expressions of ecological intelligence that have direct connections with multicultural education. It also takes account of the need to balance conserving the intergenerational traditions that represent alternatives to hyperconsumerism with a critical awareness of traditions that are ecologically and morally problematic. The aspects of ecojustice that have particular significance for how we think about educational reform include: environmental racism; the economic exploitation of the South by the North for the purposes of sustaining an excessively materialistic lifestyle; the need to renew the noncommodified traditions within different ethnic groups that strengthen intergenerational responsibility and thus interdependence within the community; and the need to adapt our lifestyles in ways that will not undermine the environment that future generations will depend on. In terms of all four aspects of ecojustice, the quality and consequences of relationships that make up the layered ecosystems we are part of is the central concern—with the correlative concern being that of conserving patterns of community life that have a smaller impact on the environment.

Each aspect of ecojustice has important curricular implications. Learning about the causes, extent, and consequences of environmental racism should be part of every student's education. Similarly, students need to learn about the modern forms of colonialism, the forces behind them, and how colonialism contributes to poverty and the disintegration of what remains of self-sufficient cultures. Knowing about the noncommodified knowledge, skills, and mentoring relationships still practiced within ethnic groups, and even within the dominant culture, is also essential if students are going to be aware of the alternatives to the industrial approach to food, entertainment, health care, education, and so forth, that requires the autonomous and thus consumer-dependent individual.

Unlike a Freirean approach to critical thinking, which represents the individual as either oppressed or as having a critical perspective that leads to changes based on the immediate judgment of the individual, educational reforms that contribute to the development of ecological intelligence and to ecojustice require that teachers possess a background knowledge of how key aspects of culture, both modern and traditional, impact the environment. These include an in-depth understanding of the complex nature of tradition, technology, language, science, and the various expressions of commodification. Without understanding these aspects of culture, particularly in terms of how they are interpreted by promoters of modernization and economic development, teachers will be more likely to reinforce the patterns of thinking that underlie a consumer-dependent lifestyle. At first glance, these aspects of culture are thought to be so much of the educated persons background knowledge that they are not given in-depth attention in universities, except for those who specialize in a discipline where one of the themes is integral to their field of study. It might also be thought that the inclusion of science in this list is a mistake, as most universities require students to take a course or two in the sciences. It is being included here because few university graduates, even those who have majored in one of the sciences, have studied the interconnections between science, culture, and the ecological crisis.

Suggesting that providing teachers with an in-depth understanding of these aspects of culture, with an emphasis on the differences between modern and traditional cultures, is the responsibility of colleges and departments of education may also appear questionable. I would be the first to agree that curricular decisions that reflect wisdom rather than political expediency and reactionary thinking would require that students learn about these topics in other departments of the university. The reality is that they are not taught elsewhere. Few professors of education, particularly those who are in the field of teacher education, now have an in-depth knowledge of these patterns of thinking; however, there are a variety of approaches that could address this problem, including efforts of education faculty to encourage professors in other departments of the university to offer courses that focus on how tradition, technology, and the other topics are understood in modern and indigenous cultures, and how these differences in understanding influence a culture's ecological footprint. Short of this, individual reading and workshops are genuine possibilities, even for the students starting their professional studies in teacher education.

The other reason for suggesting that these patterns of thinking should be addressed as an integral part of the professional studies of teachers is their need to learn how to make them part of the explicit curriculum. The problem now is that most classroom teachers reinforce modern biases that marginalize or completely undermine the importance of understanding how tradition, languaging, science, and so forth are central to understanding the nature of sustainable cultural practices and the need to preserve cultural diversity. It is difficult to think of any area of the school curriculum where a more complex and multiculturally informed understanding of tradition, the metaphorical basis of the language–thought connection, technology, science, and the commodification process would not be useful to the teacher. When these patterns of thinking become formulaic, fewer of the interactions that make up the ecologies in everyday life, in both the human and natural worlds, are recognized. That is, the formulaic (or conventional) way of thinking about tradition, technology, language, and so forth, functions like the map that Bateson refers to that influences which aspects of the territory (the interaction of cultural and natural ecologies) will be recognized. The exercise of ecological intelligence requires a more complex understanding of these conceptual patterns than existed in the formation of modern consciousness. Ecological intelligence is essential to making informed decisions about what needs to be conserved and what needs to be questioned and reconstituted in order for the educational process to contribute to ecojustice. It is also essential to knowing how language reproduces ecologically destructive relationships, and how the introduction of new technologies alters relationships and creates new dependencies. The following overview of key conceptual patterns is intended to bring out more fully their importance as background knowledge that classroom teachers need in order to counter the modernizing and progressive biases present in most areas of the curriculum—biases that limit awareness and thus our ecological intelligence. In short, the challenge is to rectify the conceptual maps in ways that illuminate patterns of interaction that can no longer be ignored.

TRADITION

If classroom teachers are to contribute to democratizing technology and science, as well as help students recognize community-centered alternatives to consumerism, it will be necessary to represent tradition more accurately, which will include understanding how different cultures understand tradition. The usual way of representing the connections between education and democracy is to emphasize the importance of influencing the direction that change should take. The modern bias against tradition, which is present in the thinking of Freire and Dewey, as well as proponents of constructivist and computer-based learning, leaves students with a conceptual orientation that does not correspond to how their daily lives involve the reenactment of traditions—with minor individualized variations. This bias leads to withholding the language and interpretative frameworks necessary for articulating what might be lost through the introduction of new technologies. In recent years, we have seen the economic destruction of small communities through the introduction of Wal-Mart-style megastores, the loss of privacy through the introduction of computers, and the loss of local self-determination that has resulted from globalizing institutions such as the World Bank and the World Trade Organization. The conceptual bias reinforced in schools leaves most people viewing these losses and disruptions as the price that must be paid for progress. That there are alternatives to these expressions of "progress" is not part of the discourse that the general public gets involved in.

Most classroom teachers reinforce in the minds of students that, except for holidays, traditions should be viewed as a sign of backwardness and as an impediment to progress and individual freedom. Students should be given the language that enables them to make explicit the traditions they rely on as a taken-for-granted part of their daily experience, to recognize traditions that do not correspond to today's understanding of social justice and environmental responsibility, and to understand why certain traditions are essential to civil society. Most important of all, if students do not have a more complex understanding of traditions, it will be more difficult to get them to take seriously the ecological importance of the nonmonetized traditions within both Third World cultures and various cultures in North America. This double bind can be seen in the way in which the progressive orientation of Freire, McLaren, Giroux, and other critical pedagogy theorists leads to ignoring the ecological crisis, as well as the importance of traditions that have a smaller adverse impact on the environment. The double bind can also be seen in the thinking of graduate students who return to their own more traditionally oriented cultures and promote the antitradition ideology that undermines the long-standing community networks of interdependence.

TECHNOLOGY

Our educational institutions prepare students to discover new technologies but do little to help students understand the impact of technology on individual lives, communities, and cultures. Technologies, both mechanical and social, are the dominant feature of modern life now being globalized. Yet most students leave our educational institutions thinking that technologies are inherently neutral (like a "tool") and are, at the same time, the latest expression of progress. The cultural assumptions about the progressive nature of change, an anthropocentric universe, and individualism support these totally inadequate ways of thinking about technology. Instead of urging teachers to become "transformative intellectuals" and revolutionaries, as advocated by Giroux and McLaren, it would be far more important to include in the education of teachers an in-depth understanding of technology and how to incorporate a discussion of technology into all areas of the curriculum. Classroom teachers, for example, should understand the difference between modern and indigenous technologies and how the differences in cultural mythopoetic narratives influence how technologies are understood and used. They should also be able to help students recognize how different forms of technology affect relationships, empower and deskill, influence language and thought processes, and undermine the mythopoetic narratives that are the basis of moral values and self-identity.

For example, genocentrism, the new metaphor that represents the gene as playing a pivotal role in determining life processes (including thought and values), involves the use of a wide range of technologies that are shifting power and economic relationships in fundamentally new ways. The experts using these new technologies, and who have adopted the progressive/corporate ideology, are now making decisions about what constitutes the normal person. They are also radically changing traditional ideas about individual responsibility. Further reasons for concern include recent experiments that resulted in gene-line changes in newborn babies and the prospect of human cloning—just two of the areas of genetic technology that signal the reemergence of the eugenics movement we witnessed in the early part of the last century. The lack of debate within the general public about the wide range of experiments with the genetic basis of life, which are legitimated on the grounds that technological innovations are inherently progressive in nature, is further evidence of the failure of our educational institutions to clarify the cultural and moral implications of technological innovation, as well as how different forms of technology reduce our chances of long-term survival. Ironically, it is the technologists and scientists who are turning out to be the transformative intellectuals and radical revolutionaries rather than the teachers that Freire and his followers envision as emancipating us from oppressive and backward traditions. And this is exactly what modern technology and corporate values are doing. The problem is that the traditions we are being emancipated from are the traditions that limit our need to depend on expert systems and the marketplace.

LANGUAGE

Like tradition and technology, languaging processes are so much a part of daily experience that they go largely unnoticed. To use the ancient Greek metaphor of "oikos," their role in managing the household is largely taken for granted. And like traditions and technology, schools and universities socialize students to a way of thinking about language that fundamentally misrepresents how language encodes a cultural group's way of thinking that, in turn, influences the individual's thinking and values. This misrepresentation, which is perpetuated by Freire, Dewey, and more technicist-oriented educational reformers, is that individuals use language to express their *own* ideas. For Freire, the source of oppression is in using language that encodes the ideas and values of others; thus liberation is achieved in naming the world for oneself. The sacred cow of most academics and classroom teachers who have a traditional subject orientation is that language serves as a "conduit" that enables individuals to communicate their rationally formulated ideas to others. According to this form of misrepresentation, the sender–receiver role of language is what makes it possible to communicate objective data and information.

The myth of language as a conduit is so deeply entrenched that few university graduates are aware of the cultural and historical forces that come into play in their use of language. Thus, the suggestion here that colleges of education should make an understanding of the metaphorical nature of the culture–language–thought connection an essential part of the classroom teachers professional studies may appear as naïve—particularly as most professors of education were socialized in their own graduate studies to accept the conduit view of language. The conduit view of language is particularly problematic today. For example, it is basic to the assumption that words have universal meanings, which makes the process of colonization more difficult to recognize for both the colonizer and the colonized. It also limits the ability to recognize when earlier culturally specific ways of thinking frame how current relationships and issues are to be understood. The ability to recognize how the root metaphors of a culture frame the process of analogic thinking (which is an integral part of learning something for the first time), and over time become encoded in image words such as "individualism," "data," "intelligence," "tool," and so forth, should be regarded as at the core of the teacher's professional judgment.

In recent years many classroom teachers have become aware of how the root metaphor of patriarchy served as a metacognitive schemata that influenced thought, behavior, material expressions of culture, and personal identities. That is, they have become more aware of analogies and image words (iconic metaphors) that encode this earlier cultural root metaphor. There are other root metaphors (e.g., progress, individualism, anthropocentrism, mechanism, economism, and, now evolution) that carry forward the earlier assumptions and patterns of thinking that were the basis of the Industrial Revolution—and are now basic to the form of economic development that the rest of the world is being pressured to adopt.

These root metaphors are also taken for granted by the people who write curriculum materials that range from textbooks to educational software. As students are often acquiring the language that enables them to conceptually organize and articulate their experience, as well as understand aspects of culture that can only be understood through the medium of words, the power of root metaphors to reproduce earlier patterns of thinking cannot be overstated. One has only to look at the fields of brain research, the human genome project, scientific approaches to agriculture, modern architecture, medicine, and education to see how highly intelligent people unconsciously rely on the root metaphor of mechanism to advance their field of inquiry. Their thinking has also been unconsciously influenced by the other root metaphors of progress—anthropocentrism, and so forth—that make their claims about the objective nature of knowledge a basic and generally unrecognized misrepresentation.

There are other reasons why classroom teachers should understand how the metaphorical nature of the language–thought connection reproduces the deepest conceptual and moral foundations of a culture. The root metaphors that progressive and anthropocentric thinkers such as Freire, McLaren, and other critical pedagogy theorists take for granted cannot be reconciled with the root metaphors that underlie the other cultures increasingly represented in the classroom. Contrary to the progressive idea that individuals choose their own values, a stronger case can be made that language encodes the cultural group's way of understanding relationships, including the attributes of the participants in the relationship and the moral norms that are to govern how one acts in the relationship. Hindsight enables us to recognize how the root metaphor of patriarchy dictated how attributes of men and women were to be understood, and thus what behaviors were moral. The root metaphors of anthropocentrism, individualism, mechanism, and so forth, also reproduce earlier culturally specific ways of understanding relationships, the attributes of the participants in the relationships, and thus what constitutes the moral norms governing the relationships. To recall Bateson's point about maps highlighting only certain aspects of the territory (culture, the environment, other cultures), the reliance on past metaphorical constructions that did not take account of colonization, overshooting the sustaining capacity of the environment, and the need to conserve cultural practices that represent alternatives to becoming even more dependent on consumerism, is becoming an even more critical issue. And it needs to be an issue that teachers constantly address—in every area of the curriculum and at all levels of the educational process. Managing the household, to use the Greek analogy, requires a greater awareness of the languaging processes that mediate relationships and activities within the cultural and natural ecologies. And this should be central to the professional studies of classroom teachers.

SCIENCE

Modern science has made many contributions to our understanding of nature and to improving the quality of life. Yet science, more than any other aspect of modern culture, involves a double bind that few classroom teachers recognize. The achievements of modern science have also contributed to the Industrial Revolution that continues to degrade the environment and now provides the basis for bringing the genetic processes for regulating life into the industrial mode of production and consumption. With increasing frequency, scientists such as E. O. Wilson, Francis Crick, and the late Carl Sagan claim that science is the only legitimate approach to knowledge. Along with other scientists, they are also claiming that consciousness, values, and cultural practices will shortly be explained by science. Science is becoming the principal means for legitimating an increasingly wide range of behaviors, products, and expert pronouncements. It is also becoming a major contributor to the creation of a global monoculture. For example, science is the basis of the computer technology now undermining linguistic diversity. And who dares question the way in which the powerful metanarrative of evolution that has been derived from scientific discoveries is undermining the mythopoetic narratives that serve as the basis of different cultural ways of knowing and valuing relationships? In short, scientists are turning their method of inquiry into a totalizing epistemology that undermines traditions—many of which are the basis of moral reciprocity, mutual aid, self-sufficiency, and cultural diversity. The public, not being educated to discern the legitimated domains of scientific inquiry and pronouncement, is not only silent in the face of this colonizing process but sees it as the cutting edge of progress.

The inability of many scientists to recognize when they are dealing with cultural issues outside their area of expertise raises questions about the adequacy of the education they receive. And the public's general inability to recognize when scientists have crossed the line that separates their area of expertise from areas of culture that involve community-sustaining traditions, and when to hold scientists accountable for the unanticipated consequences of the experiments they introduce into the cultures of the world, also suggests the need for radical reform of teacher education programs. We are, in effect, confronted with another double bind: the need to understand the cultural impact of science as an increasingly dominant epistemology and metanarrative and as the source of technologies that represent experiments with the foundations of different cultures. Unfortunately, this need will not be addressed by professors in the various sciences. Yet the increasing integration of the culture of science into the culture of international corporations, and the rate that the new industrial processes are degrading the environment, make it imperative that the public, here and in the Third World, be educated in ways that enable them to know when to challenge the authority of scientists.

Methodology classes in the teaching of science would seem, at first glance, to be the ideal venue for providing classroom teachers the basic insights they need in order to help students recognize the legitimate domains of scientific inquiry and when scientists are dealing with cultural issues that are beyond their areas of expertise. Unfortunately, most science education professors are educated to think in the same narrow way that characterizes their science professors. So the task of helping students recognize when scientists are making predictions or giving explanations that are beyond their area of competence falls to the classroom teacher. Often overlooked is that the basic insights necessary for holding scientists accountable do not require a knowledge of the scientist's area of expertise, which is not to say that such knowledge would be superfluous to deepening public debate on the cultural implications of new technologies. As the education of the majority of scientists does not involve the study of culture, their own as well as other cultures, classroom teachers need to help students understand the following: (a) the traditions being undermined or displaced by new scientifically based technologies such as cloning, genetically altered seeds, computers, and so forth; (b) the cultural implications of predictions of how scientific discoveries will influence the future of humankind, such as Moravec's (1988) claim that we are entering a postbiological phase of evolution (pp. 4–5), and the claim that scientists are on the verge of extending human life by hundreds of years; (c) the ways in which scientists dismiss other cultural ways of knowing and approaches to technology as primitive and backward; and (d) the many ways in which cultural phenomena such as language and forms of consciousness are being explained in mechanistically reductionist terms. If classroom teachers can help students recognize when the thinking and predications of scientists are based on the root metaphors of linear progress, individualism, mechanism, and anthropocentrism, they will then possess the conceptual basis for recognizing what is being marginalized by scientists as they justify the cultural significance of their discoveries. Furthermore, if students learn that science cannot explain the nature and source of meaning, moral values, traditions, forms of consciousness, spirituality (including what is to be held as sacred), and how the purpose of life is to be understood (which varies from culture to culture), it will be less difficult to recognize when scientists have stepped beyond the boundaries of their area of expertise.

COMMODIFIED
AND NONCOMMODIFIED

As corporate logos and products become increasingly integral to the physical environment of the school, as well as in the curriculum, students are being further conditioned to think of personal success and happiness as dependent on consumerism. And with more areas of daily life becoming dependent on consumerism, the cycle of turning nature into poisonous wastes is accelerating. According to Hawkin, Lovins, and Lovins (1999), the average American lifestyle now results in nearly 1 million pounds of waste per person per year (p. 52). Reversing this trend will require basic changes in public schools and universities. As I discuss how universities contribute to a consumer-dependent lifestyle in *The Culture of Denial* (Bowers, 1997), I keep the focus here on changes in teacher education that are most likely to help students recognize the community-centered alternatives to consumerism.

The classroom is one of the few sites in society where students can examine the extent to which their activities and relationships involve consumerism—from personal grooming to clothes, entertainment, transportation, sports, outdoor activities, relaxation in the home, and communicating with others. This would be a volatile issue for most parents to raise, as it would likely be perceived as a thinly disguised strategy to cut back on the student's weekly allowance. But doing a survey of the many ways a student is involved in a monetized activity or relationship within a day would be viewed as both legitimate and important by students. Exploring relationships between the media, the dynamics of an industrial system that relentlessly works to expand markets and continually changes what is in fashion, the impact on the natural environment, and the effects of having to work long hours to stave off being overwhelmed by debt on the family and community would contribute to developing the ecological intelligence of the student. That is, they would be learning to think relationally and critically about the "household" in the Greek sense of the word and how the mismanagement affects their lives and the environment.

As suggested earlier, ecological intelligence also involves an awareness of what needs to be conserved, that is, what contributes to a sense of well-being, cooperation, and long-term sustainability of the relationships that constitute the "household" in the larger sense. Again, the majority of students are not going to learn from their parents about the noncommodified skills, knowledge, and relationships that exist within the community and within the various ethnic groups that give the community its pluralistic texture. After learning about the basic differences between what has been commodified and noncommodified, students should be encouraged to survey the activities, skills, and forms of knowledge within the community that have not been commodified. Special attention should be given to how these noncommodified traditions are intergenerationally renewed within ethnic groups. Who are the mentors and what talents can they awaken in the students? What are the various expressions of intergenerational knowledge that enable the students to become less dependent on consumerism. What community building activities are going on that students would find challenging? These might include community theatre, chess clubs, choral groups, sports clubs, or groups involved with carrying on the traditions of craft knowledge that William Morris encouraged over a century ago as essential alternatives to the industrialization of everyday life. What are the mutual support systems within the dominant cultural groups and within the ethnic groups? Who are the healers, elders, and storytellers? Learning about the noncommodified possibilities that exist in increasingly attenuated form is a necessary first step in renewing and making them more central in the lives of the younger generation. These face-to-face relationships also strengthen the students' sense of belonging within a caring community—an experience that is lacking where monetized relationships are the ones primarily affirmed. Learning what needs to be conserved and renewed represents the affirming aspect of ecological intelligence, and it is likely to find support from many segments of the community—including ethnic groups who are aware that the spread of monetized relationships and activities also assimilates their children into the consumer mentality of the dominant culture.

The formulaic way of thinking about tradition, language, technology, science, and commodification now limits how the web of relationships that connect the individual, cultural, and natural environments needs to be challenged in every area of the curriculum. That is, a more complex understanding of the relationships and interactive patterns encompassed by these words that until now seemed to have such a simple and straightforward meaning (i.e., traditions inhibit progress, technology is a culturally neutral tool, language is a conduit, etc.) is absolutely essential if we are to recognize the ecologically destructive nature of such other modern ideas as the autonomous individual, change as inherently progressive, an anthropocentric world, the mechanistic nature of organic processes, and so on. Indeed, the thought patterns that are basic to ecological intelligence should replace the current conceptual formulas that co-evolved with the Industrial Revolution. Ecological intelligence is also important because it fosters a more complex understanding of the relationships that need to be taken into account in a democratic approach to conserving what remains of the traditions of self-sufficient communities. In addition, ecological intelligence provides the conceptual and experiential basis for addressing ecojustice issues that are most likely to be supported by different ethnic and mainstream communities. The support will be especially strong within ethnic groups and that segment of the community that is aware that consumerism has now reached a pathological stage.

The question of how to implement these reform proposals is an important one. As there are few university courses that address these conceptual patterns from a deep cultural and ecological perspective, it will be necessary to think of practical alternatives. Asking students going into teacher education programs to do background readings prior to taking their professional courses is one possibility. Most students going into teaching already have been exposed to these conventional ways of thinking. What they need to read are books that present a more complex understanding of tradition, technology, language, and so forth. Reading Shils' *Tradition*, Lakoff and Johnson's *Metaphors We Live By*, Berry's *Life Is a Miracle: An Essay on a Modern Superstition* (in conjunction with Wilson's *Consilience: The Unity of Knowledge*), essays by Mumford, Idhe, and Ellul on technology, Hawkin, Lovins, and Lovins' *Natural Capitalism*, Sachs' edited volume *The Development Dictionary*, and Capra's *The Web of Life* would provide a conceptual basis for recognizing that the assumptions un-derlying the modern interpretation of tradition, technology, and the other cultural themes are deeply problematic. Hopefully, colleges of education requiring these background readings would be able to offer informal discussion groups and encourage similarly minded faculty in other parts of the university to offer courses that would provide for a more in-depth understanding of these readings and others that might be added to the list.

Developing the conceptual basis of ecological intelligence will not be the real source of difficulty. Rather, the real problem lies in the degree to which existing faculty in colleges of education, and teacher education programs in particular, have been conditioned to think in terms of the modern cultural assumptions that underlie the various liberal approaches to educational reforms—from technicist to con-structivist and Freirean/Deweyean type reforms. A small number of professors of education are now beginning to recognize that there is an ecological crisis, and that it has implications for education that go beyond what is normally addressed in science education classes. But they are few in number and have little support among the rest of their colleagues. In spite of the general lack of support, there is an approach to reform that holds promise. And that is the cohort system that takes a group of 25 or so students through their profes-sional courses and classroom experiences. It can be organized around a particular theme, such as community and environmental renewal or ecojustice, and it only requires two or three education faculty to teach the courses. Thus, reform is not dependent on a paradigm shift on the part of the entire faculty (which would be an impossibility), but only on two or three faculty who share a common set of con-cerns and who are willing to unlearn most of what they acquired in their own graduate experience. There is another possibility that needs to be explored, and that is the connection between a cohort approach to education and recruiting into the teaching field students who have graduated from environmental studies programs. Many of these graduates are interested in going into teaching as a career, but there are no teacher education programs that address the eco-justice issues discussed here. Providing teacher education programs for these groups would address another problem that arises when students without an environmental studies background enter their professional studies, and that is a lack of awareness of how serious the ecological crisis is. Most students have only encountered media announcements of environmental problems, while their own lives have been influenced by modern society's ability to create a sense of plenitude while hiding the environmental consequences—as well as the consequences on the lives of Third World cultures and minority groups in North America.

There is a modest stirring of awareness among education faculty, but we have a long way to go. Whether enough faculty will join the effort to bring about the fundamental changes now required to reverse the downward trendlines in the viability of the earth's ecosystems is problematic. But one thing is certain. Basing educational reform on the Freirean idea that each new generation should emancipate itself from the achievements of the previous generation only succeeds in creating the type of individual who is more dependent on the market to meet basic needs. It is the opposite of the ecological intelligence that some cultures have already attained, and that we need to achieve in terms of our own traditions.

Students from Third World countries who enroll in the graduate education programs in Western universities will also benefit from this basic reorientation in how to think about teacher education. The current emphasis on the "progressive" thinking of Freire, critical pedagogy theorists, Dewey, and the advocates of computer-mediated learning, that will be encountered in most graduate education programs, can also be understood as the educational version of the "development" paradigm supported by the World Bank and other agencies dedicated to creating a global economic system. This more complex understanding of the conceptual building blocks that underlie modern consciousness will enable these students to recognize the importance of conserving and renewing the nonenvironmentally destructive traditions still carried on by groups in their own countries that have been categorized as "undeveloped" by Western agencies. The ability to recognize the many ways ecological intelligence is expressed will help them to avoid becoming unconscious agents of colonization when they return to their home cultures.

In summary, the argument that Freire's taken-for-granted assumptions about critical reflection and its role in the ongoing task of emancipation ignore both the ecological crisis and the complex knowledge systems of other cultures should not be interpreted to mean that all aspects of his pedagogy should also be rejected. As mentioned earlier, critical reflection is an essential aspect of the educational process. The elders of an indigenous culture in British Columbia who spent 2 years discussing how the adoption of computers would change the basic fabric of their community were engaging in critical reflection. But they did not share Freire's assumption that critical reflection should lead to overturning all traditions in order to embrace what is new and thus experimental. Rather, they practiced critical reflection within a knowledge system that highlighted traditions of moral reciprocity within the community—with "community" being understood as including other living systems of their bioregion. To make the point in another way, Freire's emphasis should have been on connecting critical reflection with overcoming destructive cultural practices rather than with overturning *all* traditions. The central role he assigns critical reflection in the educational process connects Freire with a long tradition in the West of valuing critical reflection—and with a tradition of not understanding and valuing other ways in which cultures renew intergenerational knowledge.

A second aspect of Freire's pedagogy that still has value is the emphasis he placed in his later writings on the importance of dialogue. He did not, however, originate the idea of dialogue. Many years before, Buber (1965) wrote eloquently on the differences between dialogue and monologue. Buber also clarified the fragile nature of achieving dialogue in the classroom, and that the failure to achieve dialogue in the classroom does not always lead to an oppressive relationship. Although Freire aligns himself with the tradition of valuing the educational importance of dialogue in teacher–student interactions, it should also be kept in mind that Freire never recognized the double bind of advocating dialogue while at the same time promoting Western assumptions that undermined the non-Western students' belief system. Dialogue, as Buber points out, is a noncolonizing relationship. Because Freire did not recognize this double bind is not a reason for abandoning dialogue as inconsistent with the responsibility of the teacher.

The third aspect of Freire's pedagogy that should be integral to every area of the curriculum is his emphasis on documenting the taken-for-granted patterns reenacted in the students' daily life. Freire's insistence on rectifying the use of language by connecting it with the relationships and interdependencies that make up the cultural ecology that the student is embedded in ensures that learning does not become abstract and limiting. This aspect of Freire's pedagogy is particularly relevant to the earlier discussion of the cultural patterns that need to be made explicit and assessed in terms of how they contribute to ecojustice. There is a profound difference between reading about technologies, traditions, language, and so forth, and using how students interact with these aspects of culture on a daily basis as the starting point for assessing what needs to be changed or renewed—and for knowing why. The starting point in Freire's pedagogy is the documenting of the patterns and routines of everyday life—that is, using an ethnographic approach to establish the starting point in the inquiry process. The theory (or explanation of relationships), historical perspective, and the needs to frame the analysis in terms of ecojustice issues are thus grounded in the direct experience of the student. As pointed out in the earlier discussion of the cultural themes and practices where democratic decision making is being made even more important by changes in the earth's ecosystems, contextualizing the analysis contributes to the students' communicative competence and thus to their ability to start democratizing the introduction of new technologies, what should be allowed to be monetized and coopted into the industrial model, and so forth.

Again, it needs to be pointed out that ethnographic descriptions did not originate with Freire. His contribution was in making it, rather than textbooks, the starting point in the process of learning (which does not mean that all books are a source of miseducation). It also needs to be recognized that the ethnographic description of the students' cultural practices should not be framed in a way that represents change as an ontological imperative, as Freire's writings suggest. Keeping information about our health within the family rather than as data to be shared between the workplace and the corporation providing health insurance is a tradition that most of us still value, as are other privacy rights that are now being breached by the new technologies. There are other changes connected with the new transgenetic technologies that most people, in most cultures, will want to reject—and new technologies that will also involve benefits they will want to embrace. The ethnographic description, particularly in areas that relate to the further expansion of the industrial model of thinking, may often lead to an awareness of the importance of renewing attenuated traditions, such as mentoring and the nonmonetized aspects of community life,

If Freire had examined the Enlightenment assumptions underlying his pedagogy of liberation, it is likely that his contributions to educational and cultural development theory would have been more useful to Third World activists and to educators concerned with environmental and community renewal issues. His writings would likely have had less of a messianic tone, yet would have communicated his deep concerns about achieving social justice. His followers, in turn, might have been left with a better understanding of the cultural contexts in which different aspects of his pedagogy could be utilized without contradicting his vision of eliminating all forms of colonization.

REFERENCES

Bateson, G. (1972). *Steps to an ecology of mind.* New York: Ballantine Books.

Berry, W. (2000). *Life is a miracle: An essay against modern superstition.* Washington, DC: Counterpoint.

Bowers, C. A. (1995). *Educating for an ecologically sustainable culture: Re-thinking moral education, creativity, intelligence, and other modern orthodoxies.* Albany, NY: State University of New York Press.

Bowers, C. A. (1997). *The culture of denial: Why the environmental movement needs a strategy for reforming universities and public schools.* Albany, NY: State University of New York Press.

Bowers, C. A. (2001). *Educating for eco-justice and community.* Athens, GA: University of Georgia Press.

Buber, M. (1965). *The knowledge of man.* New York: Harper & Row.

Capra, F. (1996). *The web of life: A new scientific understanding of living systems.* New York: Anchor Books.

Durning, A. (1991). Asking How Much is Enough. In L. R. Brown (Ed.), *State of the world: A worldwatch report on progress toward a sustainable society* (pp. 153–169). New York: W.W. Norton.

Lakoff, G., & Mark, J. (1980). *Metaphors we live by.* Chicago: University of Chicago Press.

Leopold, A. (1966). *A Sand County almanac.* San Francisco/New York: Sierra Club and Ballantine. (Original work published 1949)

Hawkin, P., Lovins, A. L., & Lovins, L. H. (1999). *Natural capitalism: Creating the next industrial revolution.* Boston: Little, Brown.

Moravec, H. (1988). *Mind children: The future of robot and human intelligence.* Cambridge, MA: Harvard University Press.

Rampton, S., & Stauber, J. (2001). *Trust us, we're experts.* New York: Jeremy P. Tarcher/Putnam.

Sachs, W. (Ed.). (1992). *The development dictionary: A guide to knowledge as power.* London: Zed Books.

Shils, E. (1981). *Tradition.* Chicago: University of Chicago Press.

Shiva, V. (1996). *Protecting our biological and intellectual heritage in the age of biopiracy.* New Delhi: Research Foundation for Science, Technology, and Natural Resource Policy.

Snyder, G. (1990). *The practice of the wild.* San Francisco: North Point Press.

Van Der Ryn, S., & Cowan, S. (1996). *Ecological design.* Washington, DC: Island Press.

Wilson, E. O. (1998). *Consilience: The unity of knowledge.* New York: Alfred A. Knopf.

Author Index

194 AUTHOR INDEX

G

Garcia Canclini, N., 72
Gee, J. P., 125, 126
Geertz, C., 105
Giroux, H., 135
Gore, J., 109
Gouldner, A., 123
Griffin, S., 117
Grim, J., 91

H

Haeckel, E., 161
Harrison, L., 117
Hawkin, P., 145, 170
Hochschild, A., 121
Howard, P., 72

I

Illich, I., 16, 19n.1, 29

K

Kloppenburg, T., 117

L

Lakoff, G., 186, 187
Lather, P., 109, 110
Ledgerwood, J., 105
Leopold, A., 169
Lohman, L., 118
Lovins, A., 145, 170
Lovins, P., 145, 170
Luke, C., 109

M

Macedo, 122
Macy, J., 91
Marglin, S., 6
Mark, J., 186, 187
McKnight, J., 18, 19
McLaren, P., 135
Mohawk, 25, 117
Moravec, H., 144, 183

N

Nabhan, G., 120, 121

P

Paine, R., 128
Panikkar, R., 80
Polanyi, K., 119, 120
Postman, N., 69, 123
Prakash, S., 6, 25, 28, 74, 141, 146

R

Rampton, S., 170
Rasmussen, D., 120
Rees, W., 116
Remen, N. R., 114
Richardson, C., 70
Ross, R., 141

S

Sachs, W., 6, 26, 141, 186, 187
Sale, K., 136
Sanchez, L., 62, 63
Sbert, J. M., 26
Shanin, T., 25, 26
Shils, E., 140, 186, 187

Subject Index

Printed in the United States
112714LV00002B/127-129/A